THE
Folksongs
BOOK

ISBN 978-0-634-04520-2

HAL•LEONARD®
CORPORATION

7777 W. BLUEMOUND RD. P.O. BOX 13819 MILWAUKEE, WI 53213

For all works contained herein:
Unauthorized copying, arranging, adapting, recording or public performance is an infringement of copyright.
Infringers are liable under the law.

Visit Hal Leonard Online at
www.halleonard.com

THE Folksongs BOOK

11

CONTENTS

STRUM AND PICK PATTERNS

This chart contains the suggested strum and pick patterns that are referred to by number at the beginning of each song in this book. The symbols ⊓ and ∨ in the strum patterns refer to down and up strokes, respectively. The letters in the pick patterns indicate which right-hand fingers plays which strings.

p = thumb
i = index finger
m = middle finger
a = ring finger

For example; Pick Pattern 2
is played: thumb - index - middle - ring

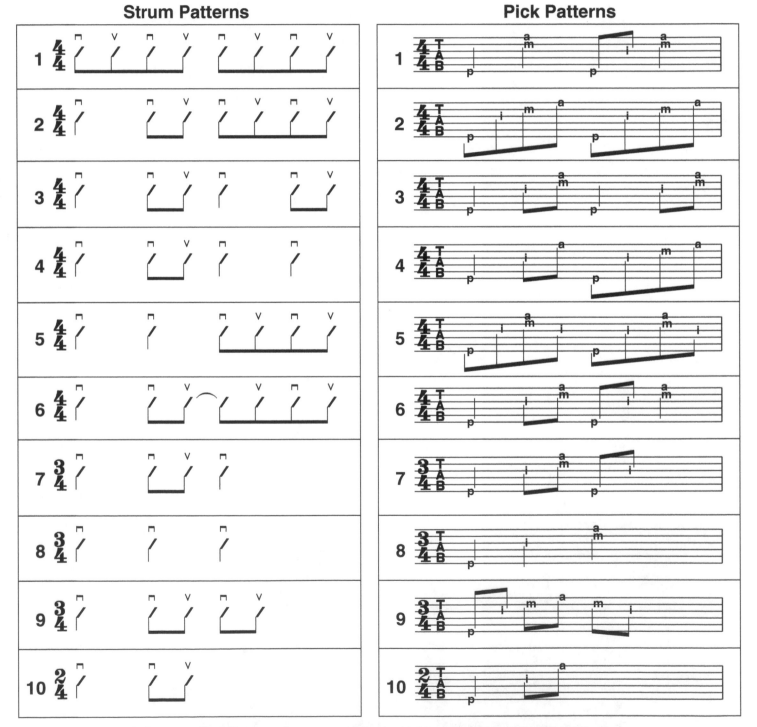

You can use the 3/4 Strum or Pick Patterns in songs written in compound meter (6/8, 9/8, 12/8, etc.). For example, you can accompany a song in 6/8 by playing the 3/4 pattern twice in each measure. The 4/4 Strum and Pick Patterns can be used for songs written in cut time (¢) by doubling the note time values in the patterns. Each pattern would therefore last two measures in cut time.

All My Trials

African-American Spiritual

Strum Pattern: 4
Pick Pattern: 5

Verse
Freely

1. Hush, lit-tle ba-by, don't you cry, _____ you know your ma-ma _____

2., 3. *See additional lyrics*

_____ was born to die. _____ All _____ my tri-als, Lord, _____

soon _____ be o - ver. _____ **Chorus** Too late, my broth-ers, _____

too late, _____ but nev-er mind. _____ All _____ my

tri-als, Lord, _____ soon _____ be o - ver.

Additional Lyrics

2. If religion was a thing money could buy,
   The rich would live and the poor would die.

3. I had a little book that was given to me,
   And ev'ry page spelled liberty.

Copyright © 1996 by HAL LEONARD CORPORATION
International Copyright Secured   All Rights Reserved

All Through the Night

Welsh Folksong

Strum Pattern: 4
Pick Pattern: 3

Additional Lyrics

2. While the moon, her watch is keeping,
All through the night.
While the weary world is sleeping,
All through the night.
Through your dreams you're swiftly stealing,
Visions of delight revealing,
Christmas time is so appealing,
All through the night.

3. You, my God, a babe of wonder,
All through the night.
Dreams you can't break from thunder,
All through the night.
Children's dreams cannot be broken.
Life is but a lovely token.
Christmas should be softly spoken,
All through the night.

Copyright © 2002 by HAL LEONARD CORPORATION
International Copyright Secured   All Rights Reserved

Alouette

Traditional

Strum Pattern: 10
Pick Pattern: 10

Chorus
Moderately

A - lou - et - te, gen - tille A - lou - et - te,

A - lou - et - te, je te plu - me - rai.

Verse

1., 7. Je te plu - me - rai la tête, je te plu - me - rai la tête,
2. – 6. *See additional lyrics*

Et la tête, Et la tête, Et la tête, Et la tête,

Play 7 times

A - lou - ette, A - lou - ette, Oh! _____

Outro-Chorus

A - lou - et - te, gen - tille A - lou - et - te,

A - lou - et - te je te plu - me rai.

Additional Lyrics

2) le bec
3) le cou
4) les jambes
5) les pieds
6) les pattes

Copyright © 2001 by HAL LEONARD CORPORATION
International Copyright Secured   All Rights Reserved

Animal Fair

American Folksong

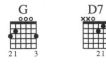

G   D7

Strum Pattern: 8
Pick Pattern: 8

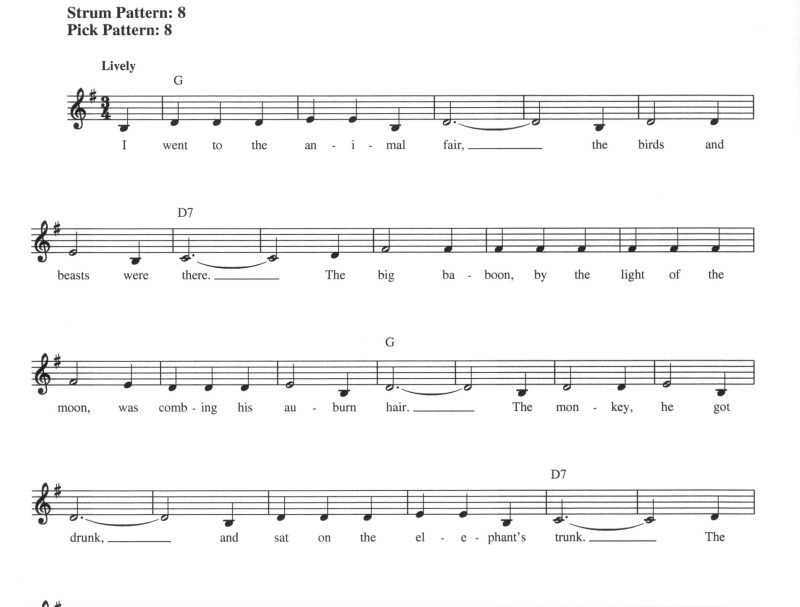

Lively

G

I went to the an-i-mal fair, _____ the birds and

D7

beasts were there. _____ The big ba-boon, by the light of the

G

moon, was comb-ing his au-burn hair. _____ The mon-key, he got

D7

drunk, _____ and sat on the el-e-phant's trunk. _____ The

el-e-phant sneezed, and fell on his knees, and what be-

G

came of the monk, the monk, the monk, the monk?

Copyright © 1996 by HAL LEONARD CORPORATION
International Copyright Secured   All Rights Reserved

Annie Laurie

Words by William Douglas
Music by Lady John Scott

Strum Pattern: 2
Pick Pattern: 4

Additional Lyrics

2. Her brow is like the snowdrift
   Her neck is like the swan.
   Her face it is the fairest
   That e'er the sun shone on.
   That e'er the sun shone on,
   An' dark blue is her e'e...

3. Like dew on the gowan lying
   Is the fa' o' her fairy feet;
   An' like the winds in summer sighing,
   Her voice is low an' sweet.
   Her voice is low an' sweet,
   An' she's a' the world to me.

Copyright © 1996 by HAL LEONARD CORPORATION
International Copyright Secured   All Rights Reserved

Arkansas Traveler

Southern American Folksong

Strum Pattern: 10
Pick Pattern: 10

Copyright © 2002 by HAL LEONARD CORPORATION
International Copyright Secured   All Rights Reserved

Black Is the Color of My True Love's Hair

Southern Appalachian Folksong

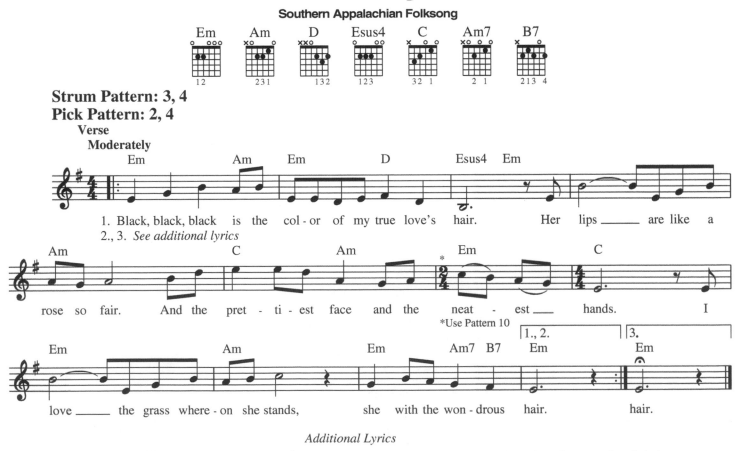

Strum Pattern: 3, 4
Pick Pattern: 2, 4

1. Black, black, black is the col-or of my true love's hair. Her lips ___ are like a
2., 3. *See additional lyrics*

rose so fair. And the pret-ti-est face and the neat-est ___ hands. I

*Use Pattern 10

love ___ the grass where-on she stands, she with the won-drous hair. hair.

Additional Lyrics

2. Black, black, black is the color of my true love's hair.
Her face is something truly rare.
Oh I do love my love and so well she knows,
I love the ground whereon she goes,
She with the wondrous hair.

3. Black, black, black is the color of my true love's hair.
Alone, my life would be so bare.
I would sigh, I would weep, I would never fall asleep.
My love is way beyond compare,
She with the wondrous hair.

Copyright © 2002 by HAL LEONARD CORPORATION
International Copyright Secured   All Rights Reserved

The Ash Grove

Old Welsh Air

Strum Pattern: 7
Pick Pattern: 8, 7

1. The ash grove how graceful, how plainly 'tis speaking, the
2. See additional lyrics

harp through it playing has language for me. Whenever the light through its

branches is breaking, a host of kind faces is gazing on

Bridge

me. The friends of my childhood again are before me, each step wakes a
See additional lyrics

Outro

mem'ry as freely I roam. With soft whispers laden, its leaves rustle
See additional lyrics

o'er me, the ash grove, the ash grove alone is my home. 2. My home.

Additional Lyrics

2. My lips smile no more, my heart loses its lightness,
No dream of the future my spirit can cheer.
I only would brood on the past and its brightness,
The dead I have mourn'd are again living here.

Bridge From ev'ry dark nook they press forward to meet me,
I lift up my eyes to the broad leafy dome.

Outro And others are there looking downward to greet me,
The ash grove, the ash grove alone is my home.

Copyright © 2002 by HAL LEONARD CORPORATION
International Copyright Secured   All Rights Reserved

Au Clair de la Lune

French Folksong

Strum Pattern: 4
Pick Pattern: 5

Verse
Slowly

1. Au Clair de la Lu - ne, Mon a - mi Pier - rot,
2., 3., 4. *See additional lyrics*

"Pre - te - moi ta Plu - me Pour é - crire un mot.

Ma chan - del es mor - te je n'ai plus de feu;

Ou - vre moi ta por - te pour l'a - mour de Dieu." ferma.

Additional Lyrics

2. Au Clair de la Lune Pierrot repondit,
   "Je n'ai pas de plume, je suis dans mon lit.
   Va chez la voisine, je crois qu'elle y est.
   Car dans sa cuisine on bat le briquet."

3. Au Clair de la Lune s'en fut Arlequin,
   Frapper chez la brune, ell' repond soudain:
   "Qui frapp' de la sorte?" Il dit a son tour:
   "Ouvrez vorte porte, pour le dieu d'amour!"

4. Au Clair de la Lune, on n'y voit qu'un peu.
   On chercha la plume, on chercha du feu.
   En cerchant d'la sorte, je n'sais c'qu'on trouva:
   Mais je sais qu'la porte sur eux se ferma.

English Lyrics

1. At the door I'm knocking, by the pale moonlight,
   "Lend me a pen, I pray thee, I've a word to write;
   Guttered is my candle, my fire burns no more;
   For the love of heaven, open up the door!"

2. Pierrot cried in answer by the pale moonlight,
   "In my bed I'm lying, late and chill the night;
   Yonder at my neighbor's someone is astir;
   Fire is freshly kindled, get a light from her."

3. To the neighbor's house then, by the pale moonlight,
   Goes our gentle Lubin to beg a pen to write;
   "Who knocks there so softly?" calls a voice above.
   "Open wide your door now for the God of Love!"

4. Seek thy pen and candle by the pale moonlight,
   They can see so little since dark is now the night;
   What they find while seeking, that is not revealed;
   All behind her door is carefully concealed.

Copyright © 2002 by HAL LEONARD CORPORATION
International Copyright Secured   All Rights Reserved

Auld Lang Syne

Words by Robert Burns
Traditional Scottish Melody

Strum Pattern: 3
Pick Pattern: 3

Verse
Moderately

Should auld ac-quaint-ance be for-got, and __ nev - er brought to mind? Should

auld ac-quaint-ance be for-got and __ days of Auld Lang Syne. For

Chorus

Auld __ Lang __ Syne, my dear, for Auld __ Lang __ Syne. We'll

take a cup of kind - ness yet for __ Auld __ Lang __ Syne.

Copyright © 2000 by HAL LEONARD CORPORATION
International Copyright Secured   All Rights Reserved

Aura Lee

Words by W. W. Fosdick
Music by George R. Poulton

Strum Pattern: 4
Pick Pattern: 5

Verse
Slowly

1. As the black-bird in the spring, 'neath the wil-low tree _____ sat and piped I
2. *See additional lyrics*

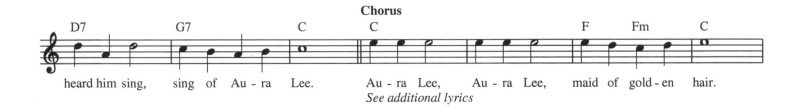

Chorus

heard him sing, sing of Au - ra Lee. Au - ra Lee, Au - ra Lee, maid of gold - en hair.
See additional lyrics

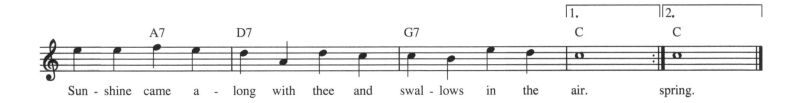

Sun - shine came a - long with thee and swal - lows in the air. spring.

Additional Lyrics

2. In thy blush the rose was born,
   Music when you spake.
   Though thine azure eyes the moon
   Sparkling seemed to break.

Chorus Aura Lee, Aura Lee, birds of crimson wing,
   Never song have sung to me as
   In that bright, sweet spring.

Copyright © 1996 by HAL LEONARD CORPORATION
International Copyright Secured   All Rights Reserved

The Banana Boat Song

Jamaican Work Song

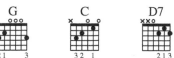

Strum Pattern: 6
Pick Pattern: 4

Moderately

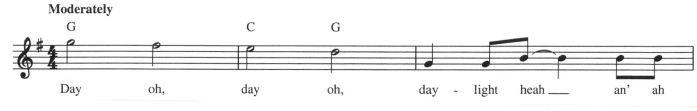

Day oh, day oh, day - light heah ___ an' ah

wan' go home. ___ Come Miss - a Boss - man, count a da ba - nan - na,

day - light heah ___ an' ah wan' go home. ___ Me work tru da night an' me

sleep tru da day, ___ day - light heah ___ an' ah wan' go home. ___

Copyright © 2001 by HAL LEONARD CORPORATION
International Copyright Secured   All Rights Reserved

Banks of the Ohio

19th Century Western American

Strum Pattern: 3
Pick Pattern: 3

Moderately

I asked my love to take a walk, to take a walk, just a lit-tle walk, down be-side, where the wa-ters flow. Down by the banks of the O - hi - o.

Copyright © 1996 by HAL LEONARD CORPORATION
International Copyright Secured   All Rights Reserved

Barbara Allen

Traditional English

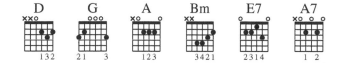

Strum Pattern: 8
Pick Pattern: 8

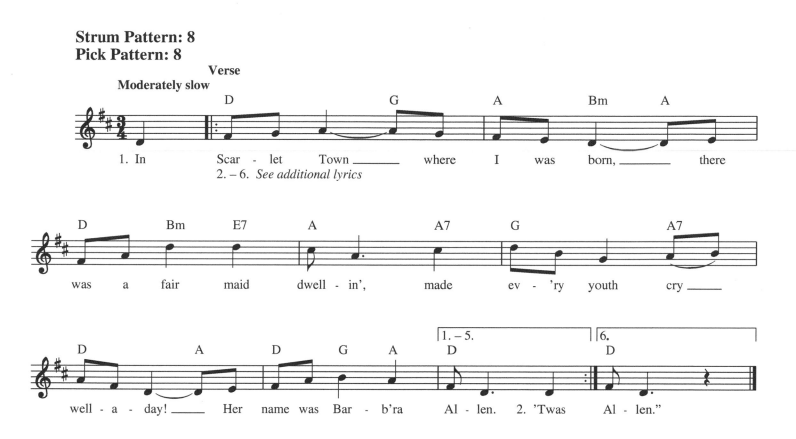

1. In Scar - let Town ____ where I was born, ____ there
2. – 6. *See additional lyrics*

was a fair maid dwell - in', made ev - 'ry youth cry ____

well - a - day! ____ Her name was Bar - b'ra Al - len. 2. 'Twas Al - len."

Additional Lyrics

2. 'Twas in the merry month of May,
   When green buds they were swellin'.
   Sweet William on his deathbed lay
   For love of Barb'ra Allen.

3. He sent a servant to the town,
   The place where she was dwellin'.
   "My master's sick and bids you come
   If you be Barb'ra Allen."

4. And as she crossed the wooded fields,
   She heard his death bell knellin',
   And ev'ry stroke, it spoke her name,
   "Hardhearted Barb'ra Allen."

5. O Mother, Mother, make my bed,
   And make it long and narrow.
   Sweet William died for love of me;
   I'll die for him of sorrow."

6. "Farewell," she said, "ye maidens all,
   And shun the fault I fell in:
   Henceforth take warning by the fall
   Of cruel Barb'ra Allen."

Copyright © 2002 by HAL LEONARD CORPORATION
International Copyright Secured   All Rights Reserved

Beautiful Brown Eyes

Traditional

Strum Pattern: 7
Pick Pattern: 9

Chorus
Moderately

Beau - ti - ful, beau - ti - ful brown eyes, _____ beau - ti - ful, beau - ti - ful brown eyes. _____ Beau - ti - ful, beau - ti - ful brown eyes, _____ I'll nev - er love blue eyes a - gain. _____

Verse

1. Wil - lie my dar - ling, I love you, _____ love you with all of my heart. To - mor - row we were to be mar - ried, _____

2., 3. See additional lyrics

1., 2., 3.   *3rd time, D.C. al Coda*   **Coda**

_____ but liq - uor has kept us a - part. _____

Additional Lyrics

2. I staggered into the barroom,
I fell down on the floor.
And the very last words that I uttered,
"I'll never get drunk any more."

3. Seven long years I've been married,
I wish I was single again.
A woman don't know half her troubles
Until she has married a man.

Copyright © 1996 by HAL LEONARD CORPORATION
International Copyright Secured   All Rights Reserved

Beautiful Dreamer

Words and Music by Stephen C. Foster

Strum Pattern: 8
Pick Pattern: 8

Verse
Moderately

1. Beau-ti-ful dream-er, wake un-to me, star-light and dew-drops are wait-ing for thee. _____
2. *See additional lyrics*

Sounds of the rude world, heard in the day, lulled by the moon-light have all passed a - way. _____

Beau-ti-ful dream-er, queen of my song, list while I woo thee with soft mel-o-dy.

Gone are the cares of life's bus-y throng. Beau-ti-ful dream-er, a-wake un-to

me! _____ Beau-ti-ful dream-er, a-wake un-to me! me!

Additional Lyrics

2. Beautiful dreamer, out in the sea,
   Mermaids are chaunting the wild lorelei.
   Over the streamlet vapors are borne,
   Waiting to fade at the bright coming morn.
   Beautiful dreamer, beam on my heart,
   E'en as the morn on the streamlet and sea,
   Then will all clouds of sorrow depart.
   Beautiful dreamer, awake unto me!
   Beautiful dreamer, awake unto me!

Copyright © 2002 by HAL LEONARD CORPORATION
International Copyright Secured   All Rights Reserved

Blow the Man Down

Traditional Sea Chantey

Strum Pattern: 7
Pick Pattern: 8

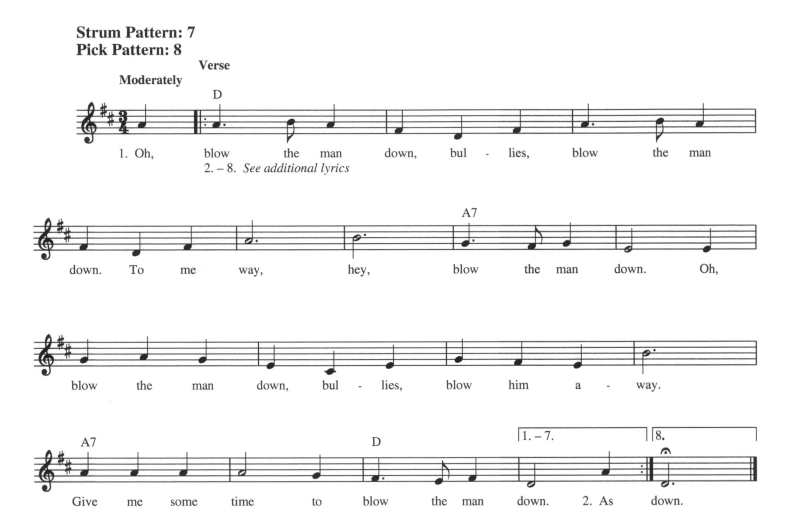

Additional Lyrics

2. As I was a walking down Paradise Street.
   To me way, hey, blow the man down.
   A pretty young maiden I chanced for to meet.
   Give me some time to blow the man down.

3. So I tailed her my flipper and took her in tow.
   To me way, hey, blow the man down.
   And yardarm to yardarm away we did go.
   Give me some time to blow the man down.

4. And, as we were going, she said unto me,
   To me way, hey, blow the man down.
   "There's a spanking full rigger just ready for sea."
   Give me some time to blow the man down.

5. The spanking full rigger for New York was bound.
   To me way, hey, blow the man down.
   She was very well-mannered, she was very well-found.
   Give me some time to blow the man down.

6. But as soon as that packet was clear of the bar,
   To me way, hey, blow the man down.
   The mate knocked me down with the end of a spar.
   Give me some time to blow the man down.

7. And as soon as that packet was out on the sea,
   To me way, hey, blow the man down.
   'Twas dev'lish hard treatment of every degree.
   Give me some time to blow the man down.

8. So I give you fair warning before we belay.
   To me way, hey, blow the man down.
   Don't never take heed of what pretty girls say.
   Give me some time to blow the man down.

Copyright © 2002 by HAL LEONARD CORPORATION
International Copyright Secured   All Rights Reserved

The Blue Bells of Scotland

Words and Music attributed to Mrs. Jordon

Strum Pattern: 3
Pick Pattern: 2

Verse
Moderately

1. Oh where, tell me where is your __ High - land lad - die gone? Oh
2., 3., 4. *See additional lyrics*

where, tell me where is your __ High - land lad - die gone? He's

gone wi' stream - ing ban - ners where __ no - ble deeds are done, and it's

oh, in my heart I _____ wish him safe at home. 2. Oh slain.

Additional Lyrics

2. Oh where, tell me where did your Highland laddie dwell?
Oh where, tell me where did your Highland laddie dwell?
He dwelt in bonnie Scotland, where blooms the sweet blue bell.
And it's oh, in my heart I lo'e my laddie well.

3. Oh what, tell me what does your Highland laddie wear?
Oh what, tell me what does your Highland laddie wear?
A bonnet with a lofty plume, and on his breast a plaid.
And it's oh, in my heart I lo'e my Highland lad.

4. Oh what, tell me what if your Highland lad be slain?
Oh what, tell me what if your Highland lad be slain?
Oh, no, true love will be his guard and bring him safe again.
For it's oh, my heart would break if my Highland lad were slain.

Copyright © 2002 by HAL LEONARD CORPORATION
International Copyright Secured All Rights Reserved

The Blue Tail Fly
(Jimmy Crack Corn)

Words and Music by Daniel Decatur Emmett

Strum Pattern: 3
Pick Pattern: 4

Additional Lyrics

2. And when he'd ride in the afternoon,
   I'd follow after with a hickory broom.
   The pony being very shy,
   When bitten by Blue Tail Fly!

3. One day while riding round the farm,
   The flies so numerous they did swarm.
   One chanced, to bite him on the thigh,
   The devil take the Blue Tail Fly!

4. The pony run, he jump, he kick,
   He threw my master in the ditch.
   He died and the jury wondered why,
   The verdict was the Blue Tail Fly!

5. They laid him under a 'simmon tree.
   His epitaph is there to see.
   "Beneath this stone Jim forced to lie,
   A victim of the Blue Tail Fly!"

Copyright © 1996 by HAL LEONARD CORPORATION
International Copyright Secured   All Rights Reserved

Buffalo Gals
(Won't You Come Out Tonight?)

Words and Music by Cool White (John Hodges)

Strum Pattern: 5
Pick Pattern: 1

Verse
Lively

1. Buf - fa - lo gals, won't ya come out to - night, won't ya come out to - night, won't ya
2. *See additional lyrics*

come out to - night? Buf - fa - lo gals, won't ya come out to - night and

Chorus

dance by the light of the moon? I danced with a gal with a hole in her stock-ing and her

heel kept a - rock - in' and her toe kept a - knock - in'. I danced with a gal with a

hole in her stock-ing, and we danced by the light of the moon. moon.

Additional Lyrics

2. Yes, pretty boys, we'll come out tonight,
We'll come out tonight, we'll come out tonight.
Yes, pretty boys, we'll come out tonight
And dance by the light of the moon.

Copyright © 1996 by HAL LEONARD CORPORATION
International Copyright Secured   All Rights Reserved

Bury Me Not on the Lone Prairie

Words based on the poem "The Ocean Burial" by Rev. Edwin H. Chapin
Music by Ossian N. Dodge

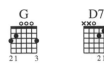

Strum Pattern: 3
Pick Pattern: 1

Additional Lyrics

2. Oh, bury me not the lone prairie.
   Where the coyotes howl and the wind blows free;
   In a narrow grave just six by three.
   Oh, bury me not on the lone prairie.

3. "Oh, bury me not," and this voice failed there.
   But we took no heed of his dying prayer;
   In a narrow grave just six by three.
   We buried him there on the lone prairie.

4. Yes, we buried him there on the lone prairie.
   Where the owl all night hoots mournfully;
   And the blizzard beats and the wind blows free,
   O'er his lonely grave on the lone prairie.

Copyright © 1996 by HAL LEONARD CORPORATION
International Copyright Secured   All Rights Reserved

Carnival of Venice

By Julius Benedict

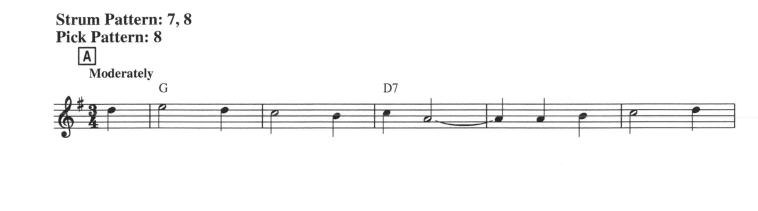

Strum Pattern: 7, 8
Pick Pattern: 8

Copyright © 2002 by HAL LEONARD CORPORATION
International Copyright Secured   All Rights Reserved

By the Waters of Babylon

Traditional

Copyright © 2002 by HAL LEONARD CORPORATION
International Copyright Secured   All Rights Reserved

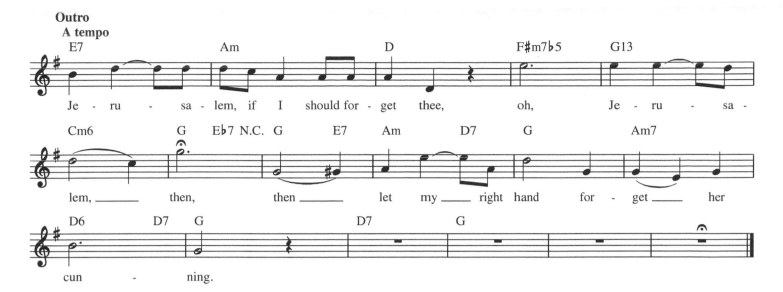

(Oh, My Darling) Clementine

Words and Music by Percy Montrose

Strum Pattern: 9
Pick Pattern: 7

Additional Lyrics

2. Light she was and like a fairy
   And her shoes were number nine,
   Herring boxes, without topses
   Sandals were for Clementine.

3. Drove she ducklings to the water
   Ev'ry mornig just at nine,
   Stubbed her toe upon a splinter
   Fell into the foaming brine.

4. Ruby lips above the water
   Blowing bubbles soft and fine,
   But alas I was no swimmer
   So I lost my Clementine.

5. There's a churchyard on the hillside
   Where the flowers grow and twine,
   There grow roses 'mongst the posies
   Fertilized by Clementine.

Copyright © 1996 by HAL LEONARD CORPORATION
International Copyright Secured   All Rights Reserved

Chiapanecas

Traditional

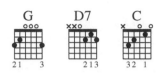

Strum Pattern: 8
Pick Pattern: 8

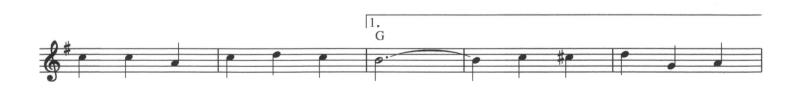

Copyright © 2002 by HAL LEONARD CORPORATION
International Copyright Secured   All Rights Reserved

Cielito Lindo
(My Pretty Darling)

By C. Fernandez

Strum Pattern: 8, 9
Pick Pattern: 8, 9

Verse
Brightly

1. De la si- er- ra mo- re- na, cie- li- to lin- do, vie-
2. - 5. *See additional lyrics*

- nen ba- jan- do un par de o- ji- to ne- gros cie

li- to lin- do de con- tra ban- do.

Chorus

1.-4. Ay, ay, ay, ay. Can- tay no llo- res,
5. *See additional lyrics*

por- que can- tan- do sea- le- gran cie- li- to

lin- do los co- ra- zo- nes. 2. U- na

Additional Lyrics

2. Una flecha en el aire
   Cielito Lindo
   Lanzo Cupido
   Y como fue jugando,
   Y fui el herdo

3. Ese lunar que tienes
   Cielito Lindo
   Junto a la boca,
   Cielito Lindo
   No se lo des a nadie
   Que a mi me toca

4. Pajaro que abandona
   Cielito Lindo
   Su primer nido,
   Vuelve y lo halla ocupando
   Cielito Lindo
   Y muy merecido

5. Todas las ilucicnes
   Cielito Lindo
   Que el amor fragua,
   Son com las espunas
   Cielito Lindo
   Que forma el agua.

Chorus 5. Ay, ay, ay, ay!
   Suben y crecen
   Y con el mismo viento
   Ceilito Lindo
   Desaparecen.

Copyright © 2000 by HAL LEONARD CORPORATION
International Copyright Secured   All Rights Reserved

Comin' Through the Rye

By Robert Burns

Copyright © 2002 by HAL LEONARD CORPORATION
International Copyright Secured   All Rights Reserved

Down by the Station

Traditional

Copyright © 1998 by HAL LEONARD CORPORATION
International Copyright Secured   All Rights Reserved

The Crawdad Song

Traditional

Strum Pattern: 3
Pick Pattern: 3

Verse
Lively

1. You get a line and I'll get a pole, my hon - ey. _____
2. - 5. *See additional lyrics*

You get a line and I'll get a pole, oh babe. _____ You get a line and

I'll get a pole, we'll go down to the craw - dad hole, hon - ey, sug - ar ba - by

1. - 4.

mine! _____

5.

mine!

Additional Lyrics

2. Get up old man, you slept too late, honey.
   Get up old man, you slept too late, oh babe.
   Get up old man, you slept too late,
   Last piece of crawdad's on your plate,
   Honey, sugar baby mine.

3. Get up old woman, you slept too late, honey.
   Get up old woman, you slept too late, oh babe.
   Get up old woman, you slept too late,
   Crawdad man done passed your gate,
   Honey, sugar baby mine.

4. What you gonna do when the lake goes dry, honey?
   What you gonna do when the lake goes dry, oh babe?
   What you gonna do when the lake goes dry,
   Sit on the bank and watch the crawdads die,
   Honey, sugar baby mine.

5. What you gonna do when the crawdads die, honey?
   What you gonna do when the crawdads die, oh babe?
   What you gonna do when the crawdads die,
   Sit on the bank until I cry,
   Honey, sugar baby mine.

Copyright © 1998 by HAL LEONARD CORPORATION
International Copyright Secured   All Rights Reserved

Danny Boy

Words by Frederick Edward Weatherly
Traditional Irish Folk Melody

Strum Pattern: 4
Pick Pattern: 4

Slowly

1. Oh, Dan - ny Boy, the pipes, the pipes are call - ing from glen to
2. *See additional lyrics*

glen and down the moun - tain side. The sum - mer's gone and

all the ros - es fall - ing. 'Tis you, 'tis you must go and I must

bide. But come ye back when sum - mer's in the mea - dow,
See additional lyrics

or when the val - ley's hushed and white with snow.

'Tis I'll be there in sun - shine or in sha - dow. Oh, Dan - ny

Boy, oh, Dan - ny Boy, I love you so. _____ 2. And when ye _____

Additional Lyrics

2. And when ye come and all the flowers are dying,
If I am dead, and dead I well may be,
You'll come and find the place where I am lying,
And kneel and say an Ave there for me.

Chorus And I shall hear, tho' soft you tread above me.
And all my grave will warmer, sweeter be.
If you will bend and tell me that you love me
Then I shall sleep in peace until you come to me.

Copyright © 2001 by HAL LEONARD CORPORATION
International Copyright Secured   All Rights Reserved

Deep River

African-American Spiritual
Based on Jushua 3

Strum Pattern: 4
Pick Pattern: 4

Copyright © 1996 by HAL LEONARD CORPORATION
International Copyright Secured   All Rights Reserved

Down by the Riverside

African American Spiritual

Strum Pattern: 3
Pick Pattern: 6

Additional Lyrics

2. I'm gonna join hands with everyone,
   Down by the riverside, down by the riverside,
   Down by the riverside.
   I'm gonna join hands with everyone,
   Down by the riverside,
   And study war no more.

3. I'm gonna put on my long white robe,
   Down by the riverside, down by the riverside,
   Down by the riverside.
   I'm gonna put on my long white robe,
   Down by the riverside,
   And study war no more.

4. I'm gonna walk with the Prince of Peace,
   Down by the riverside, down by the riverside,
   Down by the riverside.
   I'm gonna walk with the Prince of Peace,
   Down by the riverside,
   And study war no more.

Copyright © 2002 by HAL LEONARD CORPORATION
International Copyright Secured   All Rights Reserved

Down by the Sally Gardens

Poem by William Butler Yeats
Music from Irish air "The Maids of Mourne Shore," arranged by Herbert Hughes

Strum Pattern: 2, 3
Pick Pattern: 2, 4

Additional Lyrics

2. In a field by the river my love and I did stand.
   And leaning on my shoulder she laid her snow-white hand.
   She bid me take life easy, as the grass grows on the weirs.
   But I was young and foolish, and now am full of tears.

Copyright © 2002 by HAL LEONARD CORPORATION
International Copyright Secured   All Rights Reserved

Down in the Valley

Traditional American Folksong

Strum Pattern: 7
Pick Pattern: 9

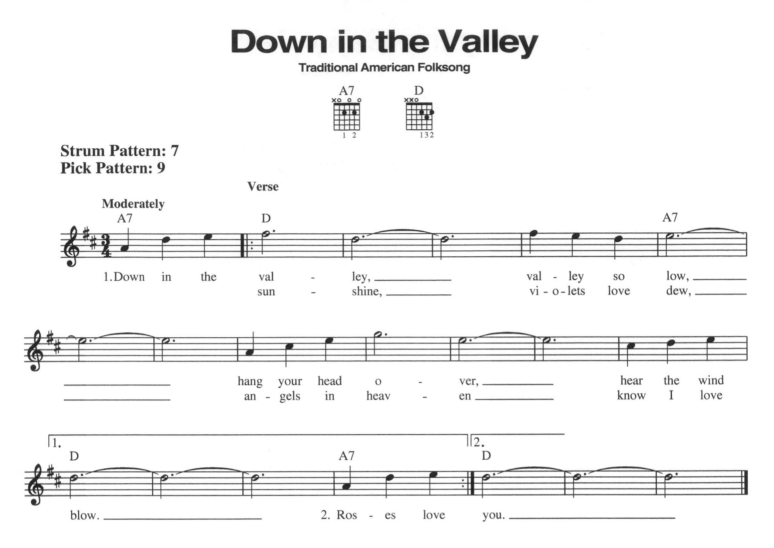

1. Down in the val - ley, _____ _____ val - ley so low, _____
   sun - shine, _____ vi - o - lets love dew, _____

_____ hang your head o - ver, _____ hear the wind
_____ an - gels in heav - en _____ know I love

1. blow. _____ **2.** Ros - es love you. _____

Copyright © 1996 by HAL LEONARD CORPORATION
International Copyright Secured   All Rights Reserved

Ein Prosit der Gemütlichkeit
(To All Good Cheer)

German Drinking Song

Strum Pattern: 3, 4
Pick Pattern: 3, 4

Cheerfully

Ein Pro - sit, ein Pro - sit der Ge - müt - lich - keit, ein
A toast now, a toast now, and to all good cheer. A

Pro - sit, ein Pro - sit der Ge - müt - lich - keit.
toast now, a toast _____ now, and to all good cheer.

Copyright © 2002 by HAL LEONARD CORPORATION
International Copyright Secured   All Rights Reserved

Drink to Me Only With Thine Eyes

Traditional

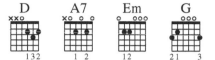

Strum Pattern: 7
Pick Pattern: 8

Verse
Moderately

Additional Lyrics

2. I sent thee late a rosy wreath, not so much hon'ring thee,
As giving it a hope that there it could not withered be.
But thou thereon didst only breathe and sent it back to me,
Since when it grows and smells, I swear, not of itself, but thee.

Copyright © 2002 by HAL LEONARD CORPORATION
International Copyright Secured   All Rights Reserved

The Drunken Sailor

American Sea Chantey

Strum Pattern: 3
Pick Pattern: 5

Verse
Lively

1. What shall we do with the drunk - en sail - or?
2. - 5. *See additional lyrics*

What shall we do with the drunk - en sail - or? What shall we do with the drunk - en sail - or ear - lye in the morn - ing? Hoo - ray and up she ris - es, hoo - ray and up she ris - es, hoo - ray and up she ris - es ear - lye in the morn - ing. morn - ing.

Additional Lyrics

2. Put him in the long boat till he's sober,
   Put him in the long boat till he's sober,
   Put him in the long boat till he's sober
   Earlye in the morning.

3. Pull out the plug and wet him all over,
   Pull out the plug and wet him all over,
   Pull out the plug and wet him all over
   Earlye in the morning.

4. Tie him to the top mast when she's under,
   Tie him to the top mast when she's under,
   Tie him to the top mast when she's under
   Earlye in the morning.

5. Put him in the scuppers with the hosepipe on him,
   Put him in the scuppers with the hosepipe on him,
   Put him in the scuppers with the hosepipe on him
   Earlye in the morning.

Copyright © 1996 by HAL LEONARD CORPORATION
International Copyright Secured   All Rights Reserved

Du, Du Liegst Mir im Herzen
(You, You Weigh on My Heart)

German Folksong

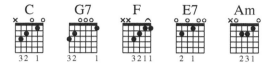

Strum Pattern: 7
Pick Pattern: 8

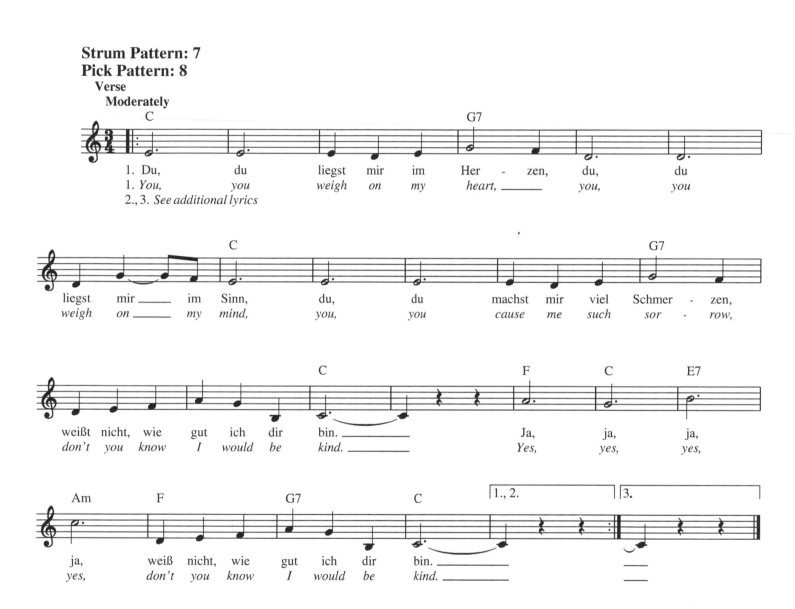

Additional Lyrics

German

2. So, so wie ich dich liebe,
So, so liebe auch mich,
Die, die zärtlichsten Triebe,
Fühl' ich allein nur für dich.
Ja, ja, ja, ja, fühl' ich allein nur für dich.

3. Und, und wenn in der Ferne dir,
Dir mein Bild erscheint,
Dann, dann wünscht ich so gerne,
Daß uns die Liebe vereint.
Ja, ja, ja, ja, daß uns die Liebe vereint.

English

2. So, so as I love you,
So, so also love me,
I will always be true,
Such sweet affection you'll see.
Yes, yes, yes, yes, such sweet affection you'll see.

3. And, and if in the distance,
You, you my face should see,
Then, then leave your resistance,
Wed me, how glad I would be.
Yes, yes, yes, yes, wed me, how glad I would be.

Copyright © 2002 by HAL LEONARD CORPORATION
International Copyright Secured   All Rights Reserved

The Erie Canal

Traditional New York Work Song

Strum Pattern: 1
Pick Pattern: 4

Additional Lyrics

2. We'd better get along our way,
   Fifteen miles on the Erie Canal.
   'Cause you bet your life I never part with Sal,
   Fifteen miles on the Erie Canal.
   Get up there mule here comes a lock
   We'll make Rome 'bout six o'-clock.
   One more trip and back we'll go,
   Right back home to Buffalo.

Copyright © 1996 by HAL LEONARD CORPORATION
International Copyright Secured   All Rights Reserved

Every Time I Feel the Spirit

African-American Spiritual

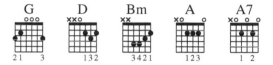

Strum Pattern: 3
Pick Pattern: 4

Additional Lyrics

2. Jordan River runs right cold,
   Chills the body, not the soul.
   Ain't but one train on this track,
   Runs to heaven and right back.

Copyright © 2002 by HAL LEONARD CORPORATION
International Copyright Secured   All Rights Reserved

Finnegan's Wake

Traditional Irish Folk Song

Strum Pattern: 4, 3
Pick Pattern: 4, 3

Verse
Moderately

1. Tim Fin-ne-gan lived in Walk-in' Street, a gen-tle I-rish-man, might-y odd. He
2. – 5. *See additional lyrics*

had a brogue both rich and sweet, and to rise in the world he car-ried a hod. Now

Tim had a sort o' the tip-plin' way, with a love for the liq-our poor Tim was born. To

help him on with his work each day, he'd a "drop o' the cray-thur" ev-'ry morn.

Chorus

Whack fol the darn O, dance to your part-ner. Whirl the floor, your trot-ters shake;

was-n't it the truth I told you? Lots of fun at Fin-ne-gan's Wake. 2. One Fi-ne-gan's Wake.

Additional Lyrics

2. One mornin' Tim was rather full;
   His head felt heavy, which made him shake.
   He fell from a ladder and broke his skull,
   And they carried him home, his corpse to wake.
   They rolled him up in a nice clean sheet
   And laid him out upon the bed;
   A gallon of whiskey at his feet
   And a barrel of porter at his head.

3. His friends assembled at the wake,
   And Mrs. Finnegan called for lunch.
   First they brought in tay and cake,
   Then pipes, tobacco, and whiskey punch.
   Biddy O'Brien began to cry,
   "Such a nice clean corpose did you ever see?
   Oh, Tim, mavourneen, why did you die?"
   "Arragh, hold your gob," said Paddy McGhee.

4. Then Maggie O'Connor took up the job,
   "Oh Biddy," says she, "you're wrong, I'm sure."
   Biddy, she gave her a belt in the gob
   And left her sprawlin' on the floor.
   And then the war did soon engage,
   'Twas woman to woman and man to man.
   Shillelaigh law was all the rage,
   And a row and a ruction soon began.

5. Then Mickey Maloney ducked his head
   When a noggin of whiskey flew at him.
   It missed, and falling on the bed,
   The liquor scattered over Tim!
   The corpse revives; see how he rises!
   Timothy, rising from the bed,
   Said, "Whirl your whiskey around like blazes,
   Thanum an Dhul! Do you think I'm dead?"

Copyright © 2002 by HAL LEONARD CORPORATION
International Copyright Secured   All Rights Reserved

Flow Gently, Sweet Afton

Lyrics by Robert Burns
Music by Alexander Hume

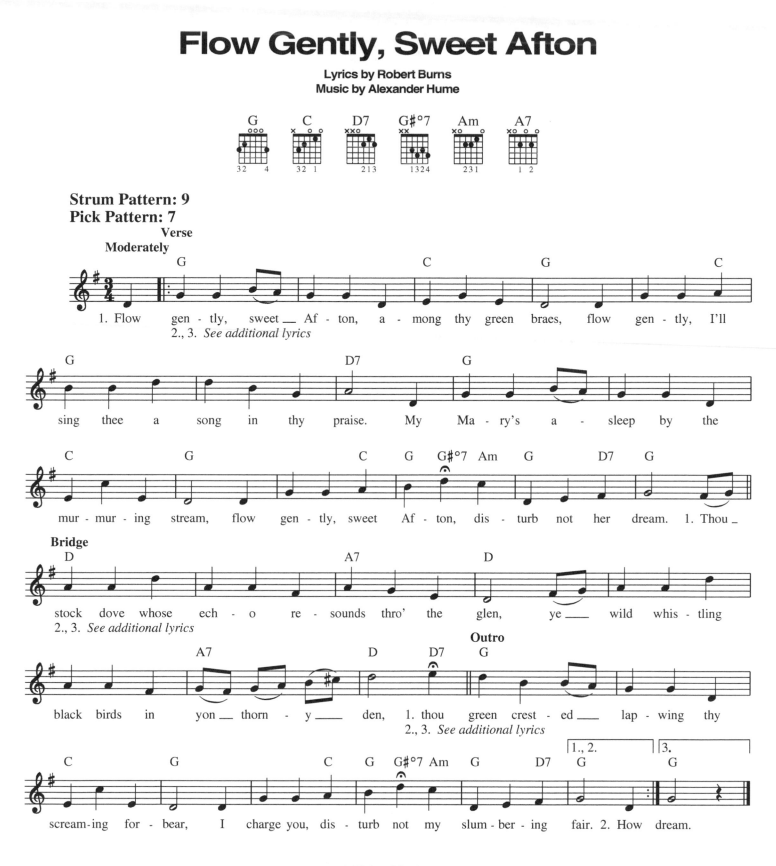

Strum Pattern: 9
Pick Pattern: 7

Additional Lyrics

2. How lofty, sweet Afton, thy neighboring hills,
   Far mark'd with the courses of clear, winding rills.
   There daily I wander as noon rises high,
   My flocks and my Mary's sweet cot in my eye.

Bridge 2. How pleasant thy banks and green valleys below,
   Where wild in the woodlands, the primroses blow.

Outro 2. There oft, as mild evening weeps over the lea,
   The sweet-scented birk shades my Mary and me.

3. Thy crystal stream, Afton, how lovely it glides,
   And winds by the cot where my Mary resides.
   How wanton thy waters her snowy feet lave,
   As gath'ring sweet flow'rets, she stems thy clear wave.

Bridge 3. Flow gently, sweet Afton, among thy green braes,
   Flow gently, sweet river, the theme of my lays.

Outro 3. My Mary's asleep by the murmuring stream.
   Flow gently, sweet Afton, disturb not her dream.

Copyright © 2002 by HAL LEONARD CORPORATION
International Copyright Secured   All Rights Reserved

The Foggy Dew

Traditional Irish Folk Song

Strum Pattern: 9
Pick Pattern: 7

Verse
Moderately

1. O - ver the hills I went one day; a love - ly
2. *See additional lyrics*

maid I spied. With her coal black hair and her man - tle so

green, an im - age to per - ceive. Says

I, "Dear girl, will you be my bride?" And she lift - ed her

eyes of blue. She smiled and said, "Young man, I'm to

wed; I'm to meet him in the fog - gy dew."

Additional Lyrics

2. Over the hills I went one morn;
   A singing I did go.
   Met this lovely maid with her coal black hair,
   And she answered soft and low.
   Said she, "Young man, I'll be your bride,
   If I know that you'll be true."
   Oh, in my arms, all of her charms
   Were casted in the foggy dew.

Copyright © 2002 by HAL LEONARD CORPORATION
International Copyright Secured   All Rights Reserved

For He's a Jolly Good Fellow

Traditional

Strum Pattern: 7, 8
Pick Pattern: 8

Moderately

Copyright © 2001 by HAL LEONARD CORPORATION
International Copyright Secured   All Rights Reserved

Frankie and Johnny

Anonymous Blues Ballad

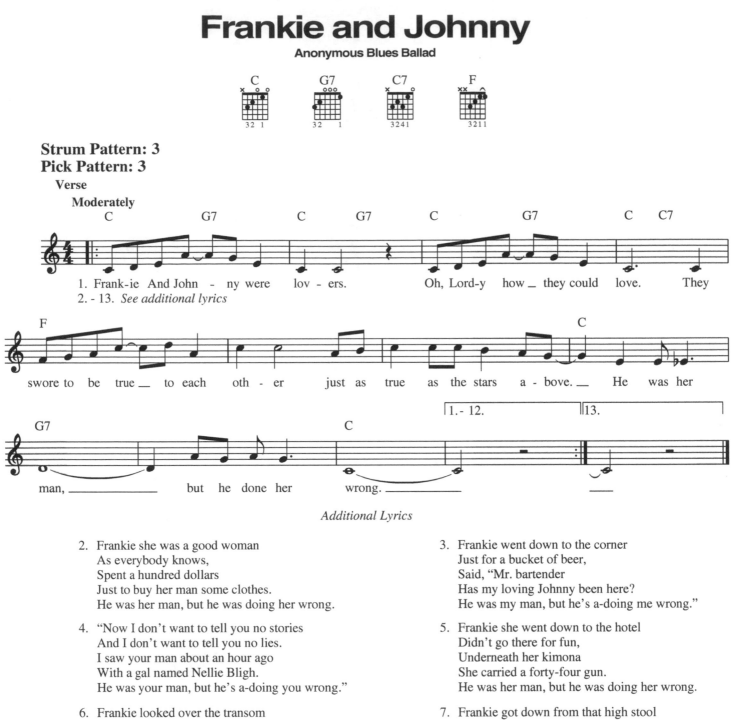

Strum Pattern: 3
Pick Pattern: 3

1. Frank-ie And John - ny were lov - ers. Oh, Lord-y how they could love. They
2. - 13. *See additional lyrics*

swore to be true to each oth - er just as true as the stars a - bove. He was her

man, but he done her wrong.

Additional Lyrics

2. Frankie she was a good woman
As everybody knows,
Spent a hundred dollars
Just to buy her man some clothes.
He was her man, but he was doing her wrong.

3. Frankie went down to the corner
Just for a bucket of beer,
Said, "Mr. bartender
Has my loving Johnny been here?
He was my man, but he's a-doing me wrong."

4. "Now I don't want to tell you no stories
And I don't want to tell you no lies.
I saw your man about an hour ago
With a gal named Nellie Bligh.
He was your man, but he's a-doing you wrong."

5. Frankie she went down to the hotel
Didn't go there for fun,
Underneath her kimona
She carried a forty-four gun.
He was her man, but he was doing her wrong.

6. Frankie looked over the transom
To see what she could spy.
There sat Johnny on the sofa
Just loving up Nellie Bligh.
He was her man, but he was doing her wrong.

7. Frankie got down from that high stool
She didn't want to see no more,
Rooty-toot-toot three times she shot
Right through that hardwood door.
He was her man, but he was doing her wrong.

8. Now the first time that Frankie shot Johnny
He let out an awful yell,
Second time she shot him
There was a new man's face in hell.
He was her man, but he was doing her wrong.

9. "Oh, roll me over easy,
Roll me over slow,
Roll me over on the right side
For the left side hurts me so."
He was her man, but he was doing her wrong.

10. Sixteen rubber-tired carriages,
Sixteen rubber-tired hacks,
They take poor Johnny to the graveyard
They ain't gonna bring him back.
He was her man, but he was doing her wrong.

11. Frankie looked out of the jailhouse
To see what she could see,
All she could hear was a two-string bow
Crying nearer my God to Thee.
He was her man, but he was doing her wrong.

12. Frankie said to the sheriff,
"What do you reckon they'll do?"
Sheriff he said, "Frankie,
"It's the electric chair for you."
He was her man, but he was doing her wrong.

13. This story has no moral,
This story has no end.
This story only goes to show
That there ain't no good in men!
He was her man, but he was doing her wrong.

Copyright © 1996 by HAL LEONARD CORPORATION
International Copyright Secured   All Rights Reserved

Freight Train

Traditional

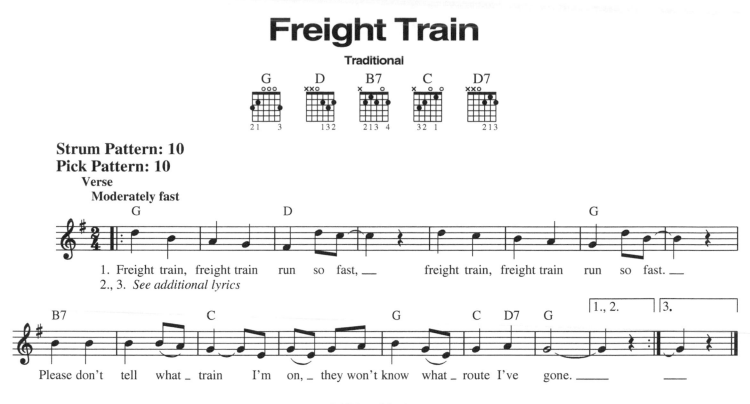

Strum Pattern: 10
Pick Pattern: 10

Verse
Moderately fast

1. Freight train, freight train run so fast, ___ freight train, freight train run so fast.
2., 3. *See additional lyrics*

Please don't tell what _ train I'm on, _ they won't know what _ route I've gone. _____ ___

Additional Lyrics

2. When I'm dead and in my grave,
No more good times here I'll crave.
Place the stones at my head and feet,
And tell them all that I've gone to sleep.

3. When I die, Lord, bury me deep,
Way down on old Chestnut Street,
So I can hear old Number Nine
As she comes rolling by.

Copyright © 2002 by HAL LEONARD CORPORATION
International Copyright Secured   All Rights Reserved

Frère Jacques
(Are You Sleeping?)

Traditional

Strum Pattern: 5
Pick Pattern: 1

Moderately

Are you sleep - ing, are you sleep - ing, broth - er John, broth - er John?
French: Frè - re Jac - ques, Frè - re Jac - ques, dor - mez vous, dor - mez vous?

Morn - ing bells are ring - ing, morn - ing bells are ring - ing, ding ding dong, ding ding dong.
Son - nez les ma - ti - nes, son - nez les ma - ti - nes, din din don, din din don.

Copyright © 1996 by HAL LEONARD CORPORATION
International Copyright Secured   All Rights Reserved

Frog Went A-Courtin'

Traditional

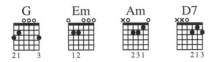

Strum Pattern: 4
Pick Pattern: 5

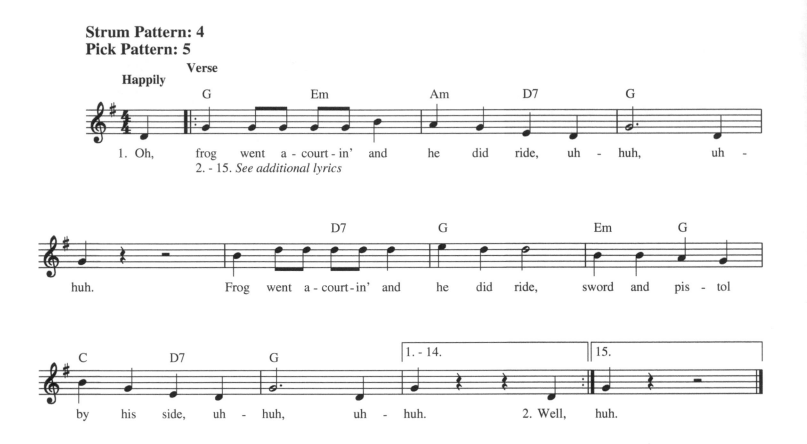

1. Oh, frog went a-court-in' and he did ride, uh-huh, uh-
2. - 15. *See additional lyrics*

huh. Frog went a-court-in' and he did ride, sword and pis-tol

by his side, uh-huh, uh-huh. 2. Well, huh.

Additional Lyrics

2. Well, he rode down to Miss Mousie's door, uh-huh, uh-huh,
   Well, he rode down to Miss Mousie's door,
   Where he had often been before, uh-huh, uh-huh.

3. He took Miss Mousie on his knee, uh-huh, uh-huh.
   He took Miss Mousie on his knee,
   Said, "Miss Mousie will you marry me?" Uh-huh, uh-huh.

4. "I'll have to ask my Uncle Rat, etc.
   See what he will say to that." etc.

5. "Without my Uncle Rat's consent,
   I would not marry the President."

6. Well, Uncle Rat laughed and shook his fat sides,
   To think his niece would be a bride.

7. Well, Uncle Rat rode off to town,
   To buy his niece a wedding gown.

8. "Where will the wedding supper be?"
   "Way down yonder in a hollow tree."

9. "What will the wedding supper be?"
   "A fried mosquito and a roasted flea."

10. First to come in were two little ants,
    Fixing around to have a dance.

11. Next to come in was a bumble bee,
    Bouncing a fiddle on his knee.

12. Next to come in was a fat sassy lad,
    Thinks himself as big as his dad.

13. Thinks himself a man indeed,
    Because he chews the tobacco weed.

14. And next to come in was a big tomcat,
    He swallowed the frog and the mouse and the rat.

15. Next to come in was a big old snake,
    He chased the party into the lake.

Copyright © 1998 by HAL LEONARD CORPORATION
International Copyright Secured   All Rights Reserved

Funiculi, Funicula

Words and Music by Luigi Denza

Additional Lyrics

2. Some think it well to be all melancholic,
   To pine and sigh, to pine and sigh.

Copyright © 2002 by HAL LEONARD CORPORATION
International Copyright Secured All Rights Reserved

Git Along, Little Dogies

Western American Cowboy Song

Strum Pattern: 7
Pick Pattern: 9

1. As I was a-walk-in' one morn-ing for pleas-ure, I spied a cow-
2. - 7. *See additional lyrics*

punch-er a-stroll-in' a-long. His hat was thrown back and his spurs were a-jin-glin', and

as he ap-proached he was sing-ing this song. Whoop-ee ti-yi-yo, git a-long lit-tle

do-gies, it's your ___ mis-for-tune, and none of my own. Whoop-ee ti-yi-yo, git a

long lit-tle do-gies, you know that Wy-o-ming will be your new home. 2. Ear-by.

Additional Lyrics

2. Early in the springtime we'll round up the dogies,
   Slap on their brands and bob off their tails.
   Round up our horses, load up the chuck wagon,
   Then throw those dogies upon the trail.

3. It's whooping and yelling and driving the dogies,
   Oh, how I wish you would go on.
   It's whooping and punching and go on, little dogies,
   For you know Wyoming will be your new home.

4. Some of the boys goes up the trail for pleasure,
   But that's where they git it most awfully wrong.
   For you haven't any idea the trouble they give us,
   When we go driving them dogies along.

5. When the night comes on and we hold them on the bed-ground,
   These little dogies that roll on so slow.
   Roll up the herd and cut out the strays,
   And roll the little dogies that never rolled before.

6. Your mother she was raised way down in Texas,
   Where the jimson weed and sandburs grow.
   Now we'll fill you up on prickly pear and cholla,
   Till you are ready for the trail to Idaho.

7. Oh, you'll be soup for Uncle Sam's Injuns,
   "It's beef, heap beef," I hear them cry.
   Git along, git along, git along little dogies,
   You're going to be beef steers by and by.

Copyright © 1996 by HAL LEONARD CORPORATION
International Copyright Secured   All Rights Reserved

Give Me That Old Time Religion

Traditional

Strum Pattern: 3
Pick Pattern: 4

Additional Lyrics

2. Makes me love everybody,
   Makes me love everybody,
   Makes me love everybody,
   And it's good enough for me.

3. It has saved our fathers,
   It has saved our fathers,
   It has saved our fathers,
   And it's good enough for me.

4. It was good for the prophet Daniel,
   It was good for the prophet Daniel,
   It was good for the prophet Daniel,
   And it's good enough for me.

5. It was good for the Hebrew children,
   It was good for the Hebrew children,
   It was good for the Hebrew children,
   And it's good enough for me.

6. It was tried in the fiery furnace,
   It was tried in the fiery furnace,
   It was tried in the fiery furnace,
   And it's good enough for me.

7. It was good for Paul and Silas,
   It was good for Paul and Silas,
   It was good for Paul and Silas,
   And it's good enough for me.

8. It will do when I am dying,
   It will do when I am dying,
   It will do when I am dying,
   And it's good enough for me.

Copyright © 1996 by HAL LEONARD CORPORATION
International Copyright Secured   All Rights Reserved

Go Tell Aunt Rhody

Traditional

Strum Pattern: 3
Pick Pattern: 3

Verse
Slowly

1. Go tell Aunt Rho - dy, go tell Aunt Rho - dy,
2. – 5. *See additional lyrics*

go tell Aunt Rho - dy the ole grey goose is dead. head.

Additional Lyrics

2. The one she was saving,
The one she was saving,
The one she was saving
To make a feather bed.

3. The gander is weeping,
The gander is weeping,
The gander is weeping
Because his wife is dead.

4. The goslings are crying,
The goslings are crying,
The goslings are crying
Because their mama's dead.

5. She died in the water,
She died in the water,
She died in the water
With her heels above her head.

Copyright © 2002 by HAL LEONARD CORPORATION
International Copyright Secured   All Rights Reserved

Good Night Ladies

Words by E.P. Christy
Traditional Music

Strum Pattern: 3
Pick Pattern: 3

Chorus
Brightly

Good night, la - dies, good night la - dies, good night la - dies, we're

going to leave you now. Mer - ri - ly we roll a - long, roll a - long, roll a - long.

Mer - ri - ly we roll a - long, o'er the deep blue sea. o'er the deep blue sea.

Copyright © 1996 by HAL LEONARD CORPORATION
International Copyright Secured   All Rights Reserved

Greensleeves

Sixteenth Century Traditional English

Strum Pattern: 7
Pick Pattern: 7

Verse
Slowly

A - las, my love, _ you do me wrong _ to cast me off ___ dis - cour - teous - ly. And

I have loved _ you oh, so long _ de - light - ing in ___ your com - pan - y.

Chorus

Green - sleeves _ was all my joy, _____ Green - sleeves _ was my de - light.

Green - sleeves was my heart of gold ___ and who but my la - dy Green - sleeves.

Copyright © 2002 by HAL LEONARD CORPORATION
International Copyright Secured   All Rights Reserved

Grandfather's Clock

By Henry Clay Work

Strum Pattern: 3
Pick Pattern: 3

Verse
Moderately

1. My grand-fa-ther's clock was too large for the shelf so it stood nine-ty years on the floor. It was
2., 3., 4. *See additional lyrics*

tall - er by half than the old man him-self though it weighed not a pen-ny-weight more. It was

bought on the morn of the day that he was born and was al - ways his treas - ure and pride. But it

Chorus

stopped short nev-er to go a-gain when the old man __ died. Nine-ty years with-out slum-ber-ing,

tick, tock, tick, tock, his life sec-onds num-ber-ing, tick, tock, tick, tock. It stopped short

Copyright © 2002 by HAL LEONARD CORPORATION
International Copyright Secured   All Rights Reserved

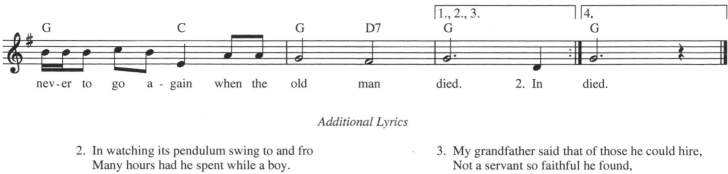

never to go a-gain when the old man died. 2. In died.

Additional Lyrics

2. In watching its pendulum swing to and fro
Many hours had he spent while a boy.
And in childhood and manhood the clock seemed to know
And to share both his grief and his joy.
For it struck twenty-four when he entered at the door,
With a blooming a beautiful bride.

3. My grandfather said that of those he could hire,
Not a servant so faithful he found,
For it wasted no time, and had but one desire,
At the close of each week to be wound.
And it kept in its place not a frown upon its face,
And its hands never hung by its side.

4. It rang an alarm in the dead of the night,
An alarm that for years had been dumb.
And we knew that his spirit was pluming its flight,
That his hour of departure had come.
Still the clock kept the time, with a soft and muffled chime,
As we silently stood by his side.

Hail, Hail, the Gang's All Here

Words by D.A. Esrom

Music by Theodore F. Morse and Arthur Sullivan

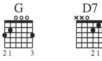

Strum Pattern: 7, 8
Pick Pattern: 7, 8

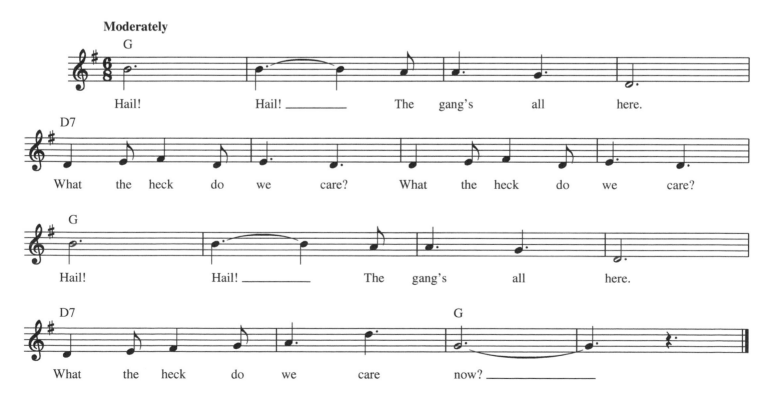

Moderately

Hail! Hail! _____ The gang's all here.

What the heck do we care? What the heck do we care?

Hail! Hail! _____ The gang's all here.

What the heck do we care now? _____

Copyright © 2001 by HAL LEONARD CORPORATION
International Copyright Secured   All Rights Reserved

Guantanamera

Cuban Folksong

Strum Pattern: 2
Pick Pattern: 4

Chorus
Moderately

Guan - ta - na - me - ra   gua - ji - ra Guan - ta - na - me - ra   Guan - ta - na - me -

4th time, To Coda ⊕   Verse

ra   gua - ji - ra Guan - ta - na - me - ra.   1. Yo soy un hom - bre sin - ce - ro,
1. *I am a plain - talk - ing fel - low,*
2., 3. *See additional lyrics*

de don - de cre - ce la pal - ma.   Yo soy un hom - bre sin - ce - ro,
come from the land of the palm tree.   *I am a plain - talk - ing fel - low,*

de don - de cre - ce la pal - ma.   Y an - tes de mor - rir me quie -
come from the land ___ of the palm tree.   *And be - fore dy - ing, I'd like*

1., 2. |3.   *D.C. al Coda*   ⊕ Coda

ro,   e - char mis ver - sos del al - ma.   mar.   ra.
to sing out my soul's vers - es for you.   *cean.*

Additional Lyrics

Spanish

2. Mi verso es de un verde claro,
   Y de un carmin encendido.
   Mi verso es de un verde claro,
   Y de un carmin encendido
   Mi verso es un cierro herido,
   Que busca en el monte amparo.

3. Con los pobres de la tierra,
   Quiero yo mi suerte echar.
   Con los pobres de la tierra,
   Quiero yo mi suerte echar.
   El arroyo de la sierra
   Me complace mas que el mar.

English

2. My verse is a bright green color,
   And also shades of bright carmine.
   My verse is a bright green color,
   And also shades of bright carmine.
   A wounded fawn is my poem,
   Seeking for peace on the mountain.

3. And all the poor of this planet,
   My fate I'd gladly share with them.
   And all the poor of this planet,
   My fate I'd gladly share with them.
   The rushing stream of the mountain
   Means more to me than the ocean.

Copyright © 2002 by HAL LEONARD CORPORATION
International Copyright Secured   All Rights Reserved

Hava Nagila
(Let's Be Happy)

Lyrics by Moshe Nathanson
Music by Abraham Z. Idelsohn

Strum Pattern: 4
Pick Pattern: 4

Copyright © 2001 by HAL LEONARD CORPORATION
International Copyright Secured   All Rights Reserved

He's Got the Whole World in His Hands

Traditional Spiritual

Strum Pattern: 3, 4
Pick Pattern: 1, 3

Additional Lyrics

2. He's got the wind and the rain in His hands,
   He's got the wind and the rain in His hands,
   He's got the wind and the rain in His hands,
   He's got the whole world in His hands.

3. He's got the tiny little baby in His hands,
   He's got the tiny little baby in His hands,
   He's got the tiny little baby in His hands,
   He's got the whole world in His hands.

4. He's got you and me, brother, in His hands,
   He's got you and me, sister, in His hands,
   He's got you and me, brother, in His hands,
   He's got the whole world in His hands.

Copyright © 2000 by HAL LEONARD CORPORATION
International Copyright Secured   All Rights Reserved

Hey, Ho! Nobody Home

Traditional

Strum Pattern: 2, 4
Pick Pattern: 3, 4

Moderately

Hey, ho! No - bod - y home! Meat nor drink nor mon - ey have I none.

*This song may be sung as a 4-part round.

Still I will be ver - y mer - ry. ___ Hey, ho! No - bod - y home.

Copyright © 2002 by HAL LEONARD CORPORATION
International Copyright Secured   All Rights Reserved

House of the Rising Sun

Southern American Folksong

Strum Pattern: 8
Pick Pattern: 8

Verse

Moderately

1. There is a ___ house in ___ New Or - leans they
2. *See additional lyrics*

call the Ris - ing ___ Sun. ___ It has been the ru - in of man - y a poor

1.
girl, and I, oh Lord, was ___ one.

2.
2. Go Sun. ___

Additional Lyrics

2. Go speak to my baby sister and say,
   "Don't do as I have done."
   Stay away from places like this one in New Orleans
   They call the Rising Sun.

Copyright © 1996 by HAL LEONARD CORPORATION
International Copyright Secured   All Rights Reserved

Home on the Range

Lyrics by Dr. Brewster Higley
Music by Dan Kelly

Strum Pattern: 8
Pick Pattern: 8

Additional Lyrics

2. How often at night when the heavens are bright,
   From the light of the glittering stars;
   Have I stood there amazed, and asked as I gazed,
   If their glory exceeds that of ours.

3. Where the air is so pure and the zephyrs so free,
   And the breezes so balmy and light;
   Oh, I would not exchange my home on the range
   For the glittering cities so bright.

4. Oh, give me a land where the bright diamond sand,
   Flows leisurely down with the stream,
   Where the graceful white swan glides slowly along,
   Like a maid in a heavenly dream.

Copyright © 1998 by HAL LEONARD CORPORATION
International Copyright Secured   All Rights Reserved

Hush, Little Baby

Carolina Folk Lullaby

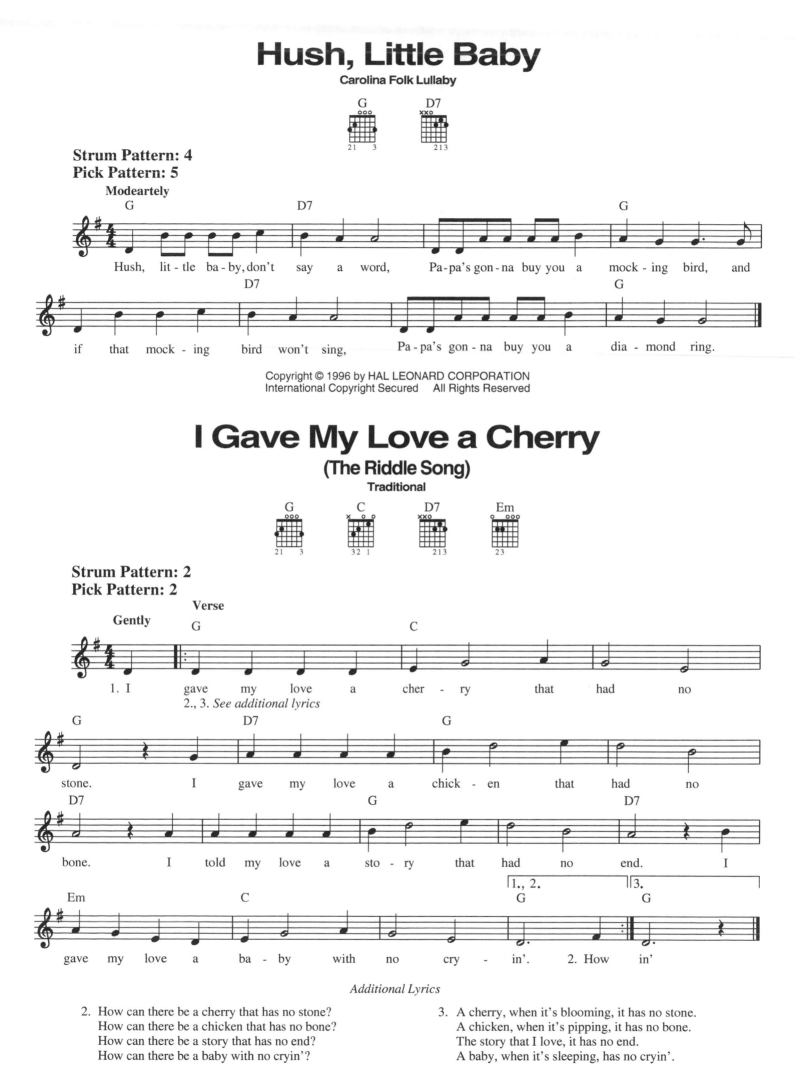

Strum Pattern: 4
Pick Pattern: 5

Hush, lit-tle ba-by, don't say a word, Pa-pa's gon-na buy you a mock-ing bird, and if that mock-ing bird won't sing, Pa-pa's gon-na buy you a dia-mond ring.

Copyright © 1996 by HAL LEONARD CORPORATION
International Copyright Secured   All Rights Reserved

I Gave My Love a Cherry
(The Riddle Song)

Traditional

Strum Pattern: 2
Pick Pattern: 2

1. I gave my love a cher-ry that had no
2., 3. *See additional lyrics*
stone. I gave my love a chick-en that had no bone. I told my love a sto-ry that had no end. I gave my love a ba-by with no cry-in'. 2. How in'

Additional Lyrics

2. How can there be a cherry that has no stone?
   How can there be a chicken that has no bone?
   How can there be a story that has no end?
   How can there be a baby with no cryin'?

3. A cherry, when it's blooming, it has no stone.
   A chicken, when it's pipping, it has no bone.
   The story that I love, it has no end.
   A baby, when it's sleeping, has no cryin'.

Copyright © 1996 by HAL LEONARD CORPORATION
International Copyright Secured   All Rights Reserved

I've Been Working on the Railroad

American Folksong

Copyright © 1996 by HAL LEONARD CORPORATION
International Copyright Secured   All Rights Reserved

Some-one's in the kitch-en I know. _____ Some-one's in the kitch-en with

Di - nah, strum-min' on the old ban - jo and sing - in'

"Fee, fi, fid - lee - i - o, fee - fi - fid - lee - i - o. _____

Fee, fi, fid - lee - i - o," strum-min' on the old ban - jo.

Kum Ba Yah

Traditional Spiritual

Strum Pattern: 8
Pick Pattern: 8

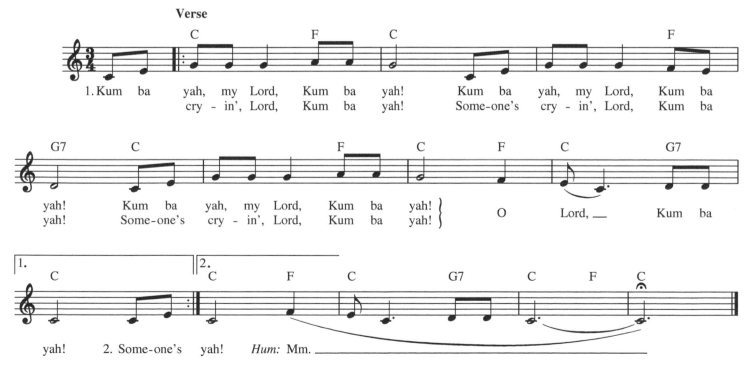

Verse

1. Kum ba yah, my Lord, Kum ba yah! Kum ba yah, my Lord, Kum ba
   cry - in', Lord, Kum ba yah! Some-one's cry - in', Lord, Kum ba

yah! Kum ba yah, my Lord, Kum ba yah! O Lord, ___ Kum ba
yah! Some-one's cry - in', Lord, Kum ba yah!

1.
yah! 2. Some-one's yah! *Hum:* Mm. _____

2.
O Lord, ___ Kum ba

Copyright © 2000 by HAL LEONARD CORPORATION
International Copyright Secured   All Rights Reserved

I've Got Peace Like a River

Traditional

C   E7   Am   F   G7   Dm

Strum Pattern: 3
Pick Pattern: 3

Verse

Joyously

1. I've got peace like a riv-er, I've got peace like a riv-er, I've got
2., 3. *See additional lyrics*

peace like a riv-er in my soul. _____ I've got peace like a

riv-er, I've got peace like a riv-er, I've got peace like a

riv-er in ___ my soul. (My soul.) 2. I've got soul. (My soul.)

Additional Lyrics

2. I've got love like an ocean,
I've got love like an ocean,
I've got love like an ocean in my soul.
I've got love like an ocean,
I've got love like an ocean,
I've got love like an ocean in my soul. (My soul.)

3. I've got joy like a fountain,
I've got joy like a fountain,
I've got joy like a fountain in my soul.
I've got joy like a fountain,
I've got joy like a fountain,
I've got joy like a fountain in my soul. (My soul.)

Copyright © 2000 by HAL LEONARD CORPORATION
International Copyright Secured   All Rights Reserved

In the Good Old Summertime

from IN THE GOOD OLD SUMMERTIME

Words by Ren Shields
Music by George Evans

Copyright © 2001 by HAL LEONARD CORPORATION
International Copyright Secured   All Rights Reserved

The Irish Washerwoman

Irish Folksong

Strum Pattern: 8
Pick Pattern: 8

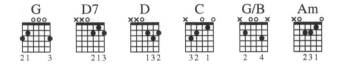

Moderately

Copyright © 2002 by HAL LEONARD CORPORATION
International Copyright Secured   All Rights Reserved

Jeanie With the Light Brown Hair

Words and Music by Stephen C. Foster

Strum Pattern: 3, 2
Pick Pattern: 4, 2

Verse
Moderately

1. I dream of Jean-ie with the light brown hair, borne like a va-por
2., 3. *See additional lyrics*

on the sum-mer air. I see her trip-ping where the bright streams play,

hap-py as the dai-sies that dance on her way. Man-y were the wild notes her

mer-ry voice would pour, man-y were the blithe birds that war-bled them o'er. I dream of Jean-ie with the

light brown hair, float-ing like a va-por on the soft sum-mer air. 2. I soft sum-mer air.

Additional Lyrics

2. I long for Jeanie with the day-dawn smile,
   Radiant in gladness, warm with winning guile.
   I hear her melodies, like joys gone by,
   Sighing 'round my heart o'er the fond hopes that die.
   Sighing like the night wind and sobbing like the rain,
   Wailing for the lost one that comes not again.
   I long for Jeanie, and my heart bows low,
   Never more to find her where the bright waters flow.

3. I sigh for Jeanie, but her light form strayed
   Far from the fond hearts 'round her native glade.
   Her smiles have vanished and her sweet songs flown,
   Flitting like the dreams that have cheered us and gone.
   How the nodding wildflowers may wither on the shore,
   While her gentle fingers will cull them no more.
   I sigh for Jeanie with the light brown hair,
   Floating like a vapor on the soft summer air.

Copyright © 2002 by HAL LEONARD CORPORATION
International Copyright Secured   All Rights Reserved

John Brown's Body

Traditional

Strum Pattern: 2
Pick Pattern: 4

Additional Lyrics

2. The stars of heaven are looking kindly down,
   The stars of heaven are looking kindly down,
   The stars of heaven are looking kindly down,
   On the grave of old John Brown.

3. He's gone to be a soldier in the army of the Lord,
   He's gone to be a soldier in the army of the Lord,
   He's gone to be a soldier in the army of the Lord,
   His soul is marching on.

4. John Brown died that the slave might be free,
   John Brown died that the slave might be free,
   John Brown died that the slave might be free,
   But his soul goes marching on.

5. John Brown's knapsack is strapped to his back,
   John Brown's knapsack is strapped to his back,
   John Brown's knapsack is strapped to his back,
   His soul is marching on.

6. His pet lambs will meet on the way,
   His pet lambs will meet on the way,
   His pet lambs will meet on the way,
   And they'll go marching on.

7. They will hang Jeff Davis on a sour apple tree,
   They will hang Jeff Davis on a sour apple tree,
   They will hang Jeff Davis on a sour apple tree,
   As they go marching on.

Copyright © 2002 by HAL LEONARD CORPORATION
International Copyright Secured   All Rights Reserved

John Henry

West Viginia Folksong

Strum Pattern: 3
Pick Pattern: 3

Verse

Moderately fast

1. Well, __ ev - 'ry Mon - day __ morn - ing, when the
2. - 8. *See additional lyrics*

blue - birds be - gin to sing, you can see John

Hen - ry __ out on the line, you can hear John

Hen - ry's ham - mer ring, Lord, Lord, __ you can hear John

1. - 7.
Hen - ry's ham - mer ring.

8.
2. When __ man."

Additional Lyrics

2. When John Henry was a little baby,
   A-sitting on his papa's knee,
   He picked up a hammer and a little piece of steel,
   Said, "Hammer's gonna be the death of me, Lord, Lord,
   Hammer's gonna be the death of me."

3. Well, the Captain said to John Henry,
   "Gonna bring me a steam drill 'round,
   Gonna bring me a steam drill out on the Job,
   Gonna whip that steel on down, Lord, Lord,
   Gonna whip that steel on down."

4. John Henry said to his captain,
   "A man ain't nothin' but a man,
   And before I let that steam drill beat me down,
   I'll die with my hammer in my hand, Lord, Lord,
   I'll die with my hammer in my hand."

5. John Henry said to his shaker,
   "Shaker, why don't you pray?
   'Cause if I miss this little piece of steel,
   Tomorrow be your buryin' day, Lord, Lord,
   Tomorrow be your buryin' day."

6. John Henry was drivin' on the mountain
   And his hammer was flashing fire.
   But he hammered so hard that he broke his poor heart,
   "Gimme a cool drink of water 'fore I die, Lord, Lord,
   Gimme a cool drink of water 'fore I die."

7. John Henry, he drove fifteen feet,
   The steam drill made only nine,
   And the last words I heard the poor boy say,
   And he laid down his hammer and he died, Lord, Lord,
   And he laid down his hammer and he died.

8. They took John Henry to the graveyard
   And buried him in the sand
   And every locomotive comes a-roaring by says,
   "There lies a steel driving man, Lord, Lord,
   There lies a steel driving man."

Copyright © 1996 by HAL LEONARD CORPORATION
International Copyright Secured   All Rights Reserved

69

Joshua (Fit the Battle of Jericho)

African-American Spiritual

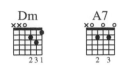

Strum Pattern: 1, 2
Pick Pattern: 1, 4

Additional Lyrics

2. Way up to the walls of Jericho
   He marched with a spear in hand.
   "Go blow the ram's horn," Joshua cried,
   "Cause the battle is in my hands."

3. Then the lamb, ram, sheep horns began to blow
   And the trumpets began to sound;
   And Joshua commanded the children to shout
   And the walls come tumblin' down.

Copyright © 2001 by HAL LEONARD CORPORATION
International Copyright Secured   All Rights Reserved

La Cucaracha

Mexican Revolutionary Folksong

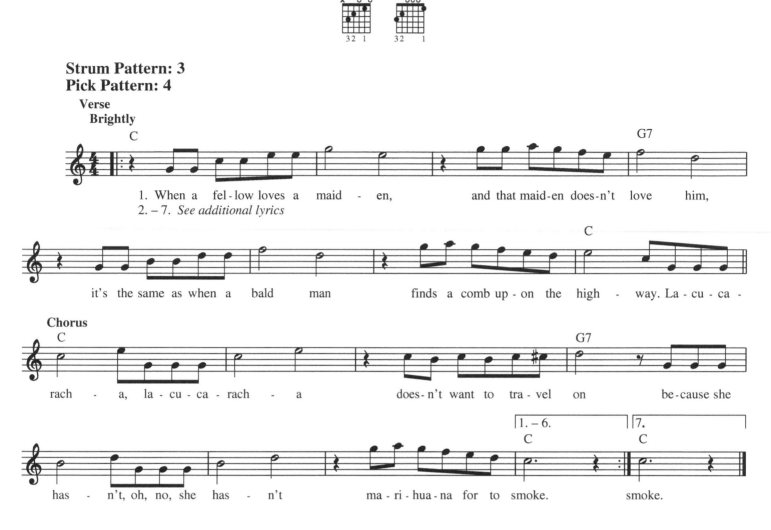

Strum Pattern: 3
Pick Pattern: 4

Verse
Brightly

1. When a fel-low loves a maid - en, and that maid-en does-n't love him,
2. – 7. *See additional lyrics*

it's the same as when a bald man finds a comb up-on the high - way. La-cu-ca-

Chorus

rach - a, la-cu-ca-rach - a does-n't want to tra-vel on be-cause she

has - n't, oh, no, she has - n't ma-ri-hua-na for to smoke. smoke.

Additional Lyrics

2. All the maidens are of pure gold;
   All the married girls are silver;
   All the widows are of copper,
   And old women merely tin.

3. My neighbor across the highway
   Used to be called Dona Clara,
   And if she has not expired
   Likely that's her name tomorrow.

4. All the girls up at Las Vegas
   Are most awful tall and skinny,
   But they're worse for plaintive pleading
   Than the souls of Purgatory.

5. All the girls here in the city
   Don't know how to give you kisses,
   While the ones from Albuquerque
   Stretch their necks to avoid misses.

6. All the girls from Mexico
   Are as pretty as a flower,
   And they talk so very sweetly,
   Fill your heart quite up with love.

7. One thing makes me laugh most hearty
   Pancho Villa with no shirt on.
   Now the Carranzistas beat it
   Because Villa's men are coming.

Spanish Lyrics

1. Cuando uno quiera a una,
   Yesta una nolo quiera,
   Es lo mismo que si un calvo
   En la calle encuen trún peine.

Chorus La cucaracha, la cucaracha
   Ya no quieras cominar,
   Porque no tienes, porque la falta
   Marihuana que fumar.

2. Las muchachas son de orro;
   Las casadas son de plata;
   Las viudas son de cobre,
   Y las viejas oja de lata.

3. Mi vecina de enfrente
   Se llamaba Dona Clara
   Y si no habia muerto
   Es probable se llamara.

4. Las muchachas de La Vegas
   Son muy altas y delgaditas
   Pero son mas pediguenas
   Que las animas benditas.

5. Las muchachas de la villa
   No saben ni dar un beso.
   Cuando las de Albuquerque
   Hasta estiran el pescuezo.

6. Las muchachas Mexicanas
   Son lindas como un flor,
   Y hablan tan dulcemente
   Que encantan de amor.

7. Una cosa me da risa
   Pancho Villa sin vamisa.
   Ya se van los Carranzistas
   Porque vienen los Villistas.

Copyright © 2002 by HAL LEONARD CORPORATION
International Copyright Secured   All Rights Reserved

Little Brown Jug

Words and Music by Joseph E. Winner

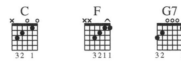

Strum Pattern: 3
Pick Pattern: 4

Verse

Gaily

1. My wife and I lived all a - lone in a lit - tle log hut we
2. *See additional lyrics*

called our own. She loved gin and I loved rum, I tell you what, we'd

Chorus

lots of fun! Ha, ha, ha, you and me, lit - tle brown jug, don't I love thee!

1. Ha, ha, ha, you and me, lit - tle brown jug don't I love thee! 2.'Tis

2. Ha, ha, ha, you and me, lit - tle brown jug don't I love thee!

Additional Lyrics

2. 'Tis you who makes my friends my foes,
   'Tis you who makes me wear old clothes.
   Here you are so near my nose,
   So tip her up and down she goes!

Copyright © 1996 by HAL LEONARD CORPORATION
International Copyright Secured   All Rights Reserved

Loch Lomond

Scottish Folksong

G   Em   C   Am7   D7   Bm

Strum Pattern: 3
Pick Pattern: 3

Moderately

Oh, ye'll take the high road and I'll take the low road and I'll be in Scot - land a - fore ye, but me and my true love will nev - er meet a - gain on the bon - nie, bon - nie banks of Loch Lo - mond.

Copyright © 2002 by HAL LEONARD CORPORATION
International Copyright Secured   All Rights Reserved

Lonesome Valley

Traditional Spiritual

G   C   D   D7   Am7

Strum Pattern: 3
Pick Pattern: 2

Moderately

Verse

1. Je - sus walked _____ this lone - some val - ley. He had to
2., 3. *See additional lyrics*

walk _____ it by Him - self. Oh, no - bod - y else _____ could walk it for Him. He had to walk it by ___ Him - self. 2. We must self.

Additional Lyrics

2. We must walk this lonesome valley.
   We have to walk it by ourselves.
   Oh, nobody else can walk it for us.
   We have to walk it by ourselves.

3. You must go and stand your trial.
   You have to stand it by yourself.
   Oh, nobody else can stand it for you.
   You have to stand it by yourself.

Copyright © 2002 by HAL LEONARD CORPORATION
International Copyright Secured   All Rights Reserved

Man of Constant Sorrow

Traditional

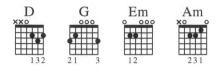

Strum Pattern: 3, 4
Pick Pattern: 3, 4

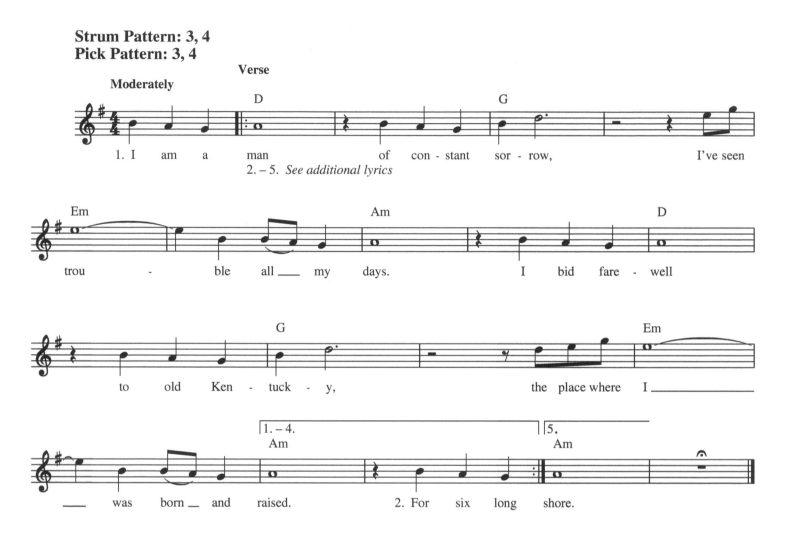

Additional Lyrics

2. For six long years I've been in trouble,
   No pleasure here on earth I found,
   For in this world I'm bound to ramble,
   I have no friends to help me now.

3. It's fare you well, my own true lover,
   I never expect to see you again;
   For I'm bound to ride that northern railroad,
   Perhaps I'll die upon this train.

4. You may bury me in some deep valley
   For many years where I may lay,
   Then you may learn to love another
   While I am sleeping in my grave.

5. Maybe your friends think I'm just a stranger,
   My face you never will see no more,
   But there is one promise that is given,
   I'll meet you on God's golden shore.

Copyright © 2002 by HAL LEONARD CORPORATION
International Copyright Secured   All Rights Reserved

Maori Farewell Song

Traditional Hawaiian Folksong

Strum Pattern: 7, 8
Pick Pattern: 7, 8
Moderately

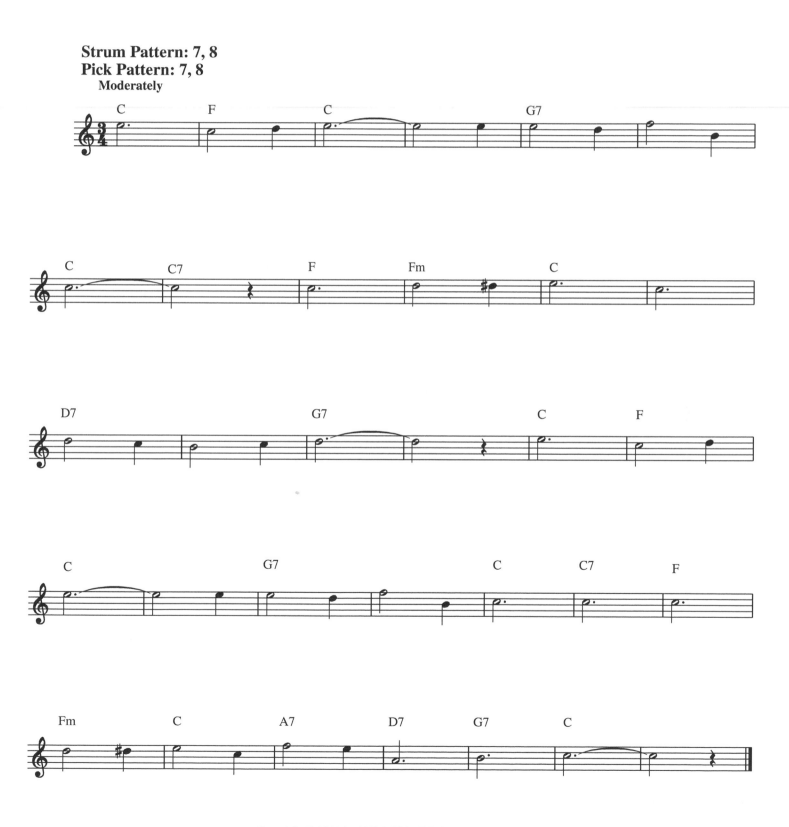

Copyright © 2002 by HAL LEONARD CORPORATION
International Copyright Secured   All Rights Reserved

Marianne

Traditional

A   E7

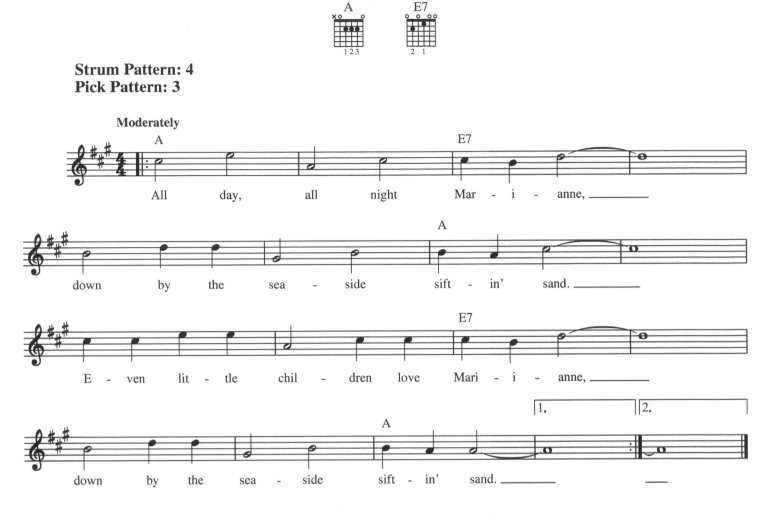

Strum Pattern: 4
Pick Pattern: 3

All day, all night Mar - i - anne, _____

down by the sea - side sift - in' sand. _____

E - ven lit - tle chil - dren love Mari - i - anne, _____

down by the sea - side sift - in' sand. _____

Copyright © 2001 by HAL LEONARD CORPORATION
International Copyright Secured   All Rights Reserved

Mrs. Murphy's Chowder

Irish Folksong

G   D   D7   Am

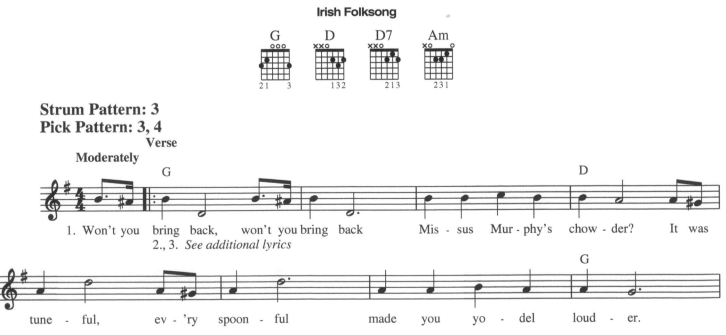

Strum Pattern: 3
Pick Pattern: 3, 4

1. Won't you bring back, won't you bring back Mis - sus Mur - phy's chow - der? It was
2., 3. *See additional lyrics*

tune - ful, ev - 'ry spoon - ful made you yo - del loud - er.

Copyright © 2002 by HAL LEONARD CORPORATION
International Copyright Secured   All Rights Reserved

Additional Lyrics

2. Won't you bring back, won't you bring back Missus Murphy's chowder?
From each helping, you'll be yelping for a headache powder.
And if they had it where you are,
You might find an Austin car in a plate of Missus Murphy's chowder.

3. Won't you bring back, won't you bring back Missus Murphy's chowder?
You can pack it, you can stack it all around the larder.
The plumber died the other day;
They embalmed him right away in a bowl of Missus Murphy's chowder.

Matilda

Traditional Folksong

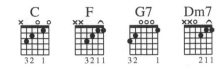

Strum Pattern: 4, 3
Pick Pattern: 4, 3

Chorus
Brightly

Ma - til - da, _____ Ma - til - da, _____

Ma - til - da, she took me mon - ey and run Ven - e - zue - la! _____ 1. That

Verse

wom - an made a wreck of me.
2., 3., 4. *See additional lyrics*

What she done to me you

ought to see. ___ Ma - til - da, she take me mon - ey and

gone Ven - e - zue - la! _____

Additional Lyrics

2. I save up, gonna make her my wife.
   But she wanta live another kind of life.
   Matilda, she take me money and gone Venezuela!

3. We were sleepin' in me bed,
   When she found the money me had hid.
   Matilda, she take me money and gone Venezuela!

4. What to do and where to go,
   Never trust a woman with your dough.
   Matilda, she take me money and gone Venezuela!

Copyright © 2002 by HAL LEONARD CORPORATION
International Copyright Secured   All Rights Reserved

Michael Row the Boat Ashore

Traditional Folksong

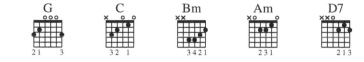

Strum Pattern: 3
Pick Pattern: 3

Additional Lyrics

2. Jordan River is chilly and cold, hallelujah.
   Kills the body but not the soul, halleljah.

3. Jordan River is deep and wide, hallelujah.
   Milk and honey on the other side, hallelujah.

Copyright © 2001 by HAL LEONARD CORPORATION
International Copyright Secured   All Rights Reserved

Midnight Special

Railroad Song

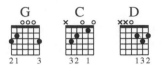

Strum Pattern: 2, 3
Pick Pattern: 3, 4

1. Well, you wake up in the morn - ing, hear the ding _ dong ring,
2., 3. *See additional lyrics*

you go march-ing to the ta - ble, see the same _ damn _ thing.

Well, it's on - ly one _ ta - ble, knife and fork _ and a pan,

and if you say a thing a - bout it, you're in trou-ble with the man. Let the Mid - night

Chorus

Spe - cial shine her light _ on me. Let the Mid - night

Spe - cial shine her ev - er lov - in' light on me. _

Additional Lyrics

2. If you ever go to Houston, you'd better walk right,
And you better not stagger, and you better not fight.
'Cause the Sheriff will arrest you, and he'll carry you down,
And you can bet your bottom dollar, you're for Sugarland bound.

3. Lord, Thelma said she loved me, but I believe she told a lie,
'Cause she hasn't been to see me since last July.
She brought me little coffee, she brought me little tea,
She brought me nearly ev'rything but the jailhouse key.

Copyright © 2002 by HAL LEONARD CORPORATION
International Copyright Secured   All Rights Reserved

Molly Malone
(Cockles & Mussels)

Irish Folksong

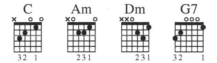

Strum Pattern: 7, 8
Pick Pattern: 9

Additional Lyrics

2. She was a fish monger, but sure was no wonder,
   For so were her mother and father before.
   They drove their wheel barrows
   Through streets broad and narrow
   Crying, "Cockles and mussels, alive, alive-o.
   Alive, alive-o, alive, alive-o,"
   Crying, "Cockles and mussels, alive, alive-o."

3. She died of a fever, and nothing could save her,
   And that was the end of sweet Molly Malone.
   Her ghost wheels a barrow
   Through streets broad and narrow,
   Crying, "Cockles and mussels, alive, alive-o.
   Alive, alive-o, alive, alive-o,"
   Crying, "Cockles and mussels, alive, alive-o."

Copyright © 2002 by HAL LEONARD CORPORATION
International Copyright Secured   All Rights Reserved

My Bonnie Lies Over the Ocean

Traditional

Copyright © 1998 by HAL LEONARD CORPORATION
International Copyright Secured   All Rights Reserved

My Old Kentucky Home

Words and Music by Stephen C. Foster

C   F   D7   G7

Strum Pattern: 5
Pick Pattern: 5

℅ **Verse**

Slowly

C   F   C   D7

1. The sun shines bright on my old Ken-tuck-y home. 'Tis sum-mer the work-ers are
2. - 6. *See additional lyrics*

G7   C   F   C

gay.   The corn-top's ripe and the mea-dow's in bloom while the

1., 3., 5.

G7   F   C

birds make mu-sic all the day.

2., 4., 6.

C   G7   C

2. The old Ken-tuck-y home, good night.

Chorus

C   F   C   F   C

Weep no more, my la-dy, oh, __ weep no more to-day. We will sing one song for my

last time, to Coda ⊕   *D.S. al Coda*   ⊕ *Coda*
                                   (take repeats)

F   C   G7   C   C

old Ken-tuck-y home, for my old Ken-tuck-y home far a-way.   way.

Additional Lyrics

2. The young folks roll on the little cabin floor
   All merry, all happy and bright.
   By'n by hard times comes a-knocking at the door,
   Then my old Kentucky home, good night.

3. They hunt no more for the possum and the coon
   On meadow, the hill and the shore.
   They sing no more by the glimmer of the moon
   On the bench by that old cabin door.

4. The day goes by like a shadow o'er the heart,
   With sorrow where all was delight.
   The time has come when the good folks have to part,
   Then my old Kentucky home, good night.

5. The head must bow and the back will have to bend
   Wherever the poor folks may go.
   A few more days and the trouble will end
   In the field where the sugarcanes may grow.

6. A few more days for to tote the weary load.
   No matter, 'twill never by light.
   A few more days till we totter on the road,
   Then my old Kentucky home, good night.

Copyright © 1996 by HAL LEONARD CORPORATION
International Copyright Secured   All Rights Reserved

My Wild Irish Rose

Words and Music by Chauncey Olcott

Strum Pattern: 7, 9
Pick Pattern: 8

Copyright © 2001 by HAL LEONARD CORPORATION
International Copyright Secured   All Rights Reserved

Additional Lyrics

2. They may sing of their roses, which by other names,
   Would smell just as sweetly, they say,
   But I know that my rose would never consent
   To have that sweet name taken away.
   Her glances are shy when e'er I pass by
   The bower where my true love grows.

Nobody Knows the Trouble I've Seen

African-American Spiritual

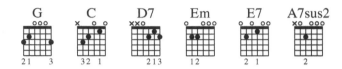

Strum Pattern: 3
Pick Pattern: 2

Copyright © 2002 by HAL LEONARD CORPORATION
International Copyright Secured   All Rights Reserved

Oh Mary Don't You Weep

Traditional Spiritual

Additional Lyrics

2. Wonder what Satan's grumblin' 'bout,
   Chained in hell and he can't get out.
   Pharoah's army got drownded.
   Oh Mary, don't you weep.

3. Satan's mad and I am glad,
   Missed that soul he thought he had.
   Pharoah's army got drownded.
   Oh Mary, don't you weep.

4. I went down in the valley to pray,
   My soul got happy and stayed all day.
   Pharoah's army got drownded.
   Oh Mary, don't you weep.

Copyright © 2002 by HAL LEONARD CORPORATION
International Copyright Secured   All Rights Reserved

Oh! Susanna

Words and Music by Stephen C. Foster

Strum Pattern: 3
Pick Pattern: 4

Additional Lyrics

2. It rained all night the day I left,
   The weather it was dry.
   The sun so hot I froze to death,
   Susanna don't you cry.

3. I had a dream the other night
   When everything was still.
   I thought I saw Susanna
   A-coming down the hill.

4. The buckwheat cake was in her mouth
   The tear was in her eye.
   Say I, "I'm coming from the South,
   Susanna, don't you cry."

Copyright © 1996 by HAL LEONARD CORPORATION
International Copyright Secured   All Rights Reserved

The Old Gray Mare

Words and Music by J. Warner

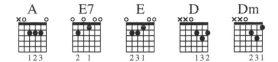

Strum Pattern: 2
Pick Pattern: 4

Moderately

Copyright © 2002 by HAL LEONARD CORPORATION
International Copyright Secured   All Rights Reserved

Oh, Them Golden Slippers

Words and Music by James A. Bland

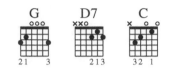

Strum Pattern: 2
Pick Pattern: 3

1. Oh, my gold-en slip-pers are ___ laid a-way, 'cause I don't 'spect to wear 'em 'til my
2., 3. *See additional lyrics*

wed-ding day, and my long-tailed coat that I love so well, I will wear up in the char-iot in the

morn. And my long white robe ___ that I bought last June, I'm ___ goin' to get changed 'case it

fits too soon, and the ole gray horse that I used to drive, I will hitch him to the char-iot in the

morn. Oh, them gold-en slip-pers! Oh, them gold-en slip-pers!

Copyright © 2002 by HAL LEONARD CORPORATION
International Copyright Secured   All Rights Reserved

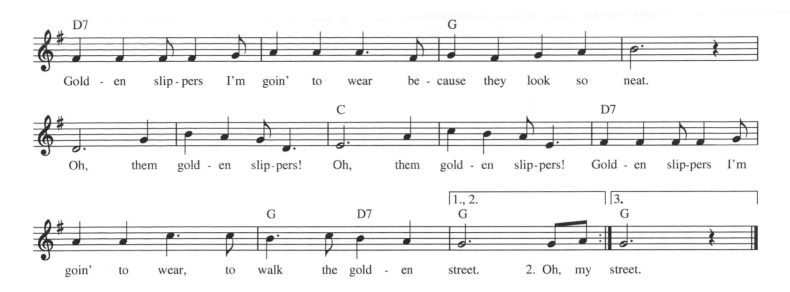

Golden slippers I'm goin' to wear because they look so neat.

Oh, them golden slippers! Oh, them golden slippers! Golden slippers I'm

goin' to wear, to walk the golden street. 2. Oh, my street.

Additional Lyrics

2. Oh, my old banjo hangs on the wall,
  'Cause it ain't been tuned since way last fall,
  But the folks all say we will have a good time,
  When we ride up in the chariot in the morn.
  There's old Brother Ben and Sister Luce,
  They will telegraph the news to Uncle 'Bacco Juice,
  What a great camp meetin' there will be that day,
  When we ride up in the chariot in the morn.

3. So, it's goodbye children, I will have to go,
  Where the rain don't fall and the wind don't blow,
  And your ulster coats, why, you will not need,
  When you ride up in the chariot in the morn.
  But your golden slippers must be nice and clean,
  And your age must be just sweet sixteen,
  And you're white kid gloves you will have to wear,
  When you ride up in the chariot in the morn.

Old Joe Clark

Tennessee Folksong

Strum Pattern: 10
Pick Pattern: 10

1. Old Joe Clark, he had a house, six-teen sto-ries high. Ev-'ry sto-ry
2. - 4. *See additional lyrics*

in the house smelled like ap-ple pie. 'Round and 'round, old Joe Clark,

'round and 'round, I says. 'Round and 'round, old Joe Clark, dance your cares a-way. way!

Additional Lyrics

2. I went up to Joe's new house,
  Stepped right in the door.
  Joe was sleepin' on a feather bed,
  I had to sleep on the floor.

3. Old Joe Clark he had a dog,
  Dumb as he could be.
  Barked a ladybug up a stump,
  A pig up a hollow tree.

4. Old Joe Clark had a mean old cat,
  Never did sing or pray.
  Stuck her head in the milking pail,
  Washed her sins away!

Copyright © 1996 by HAL LEONARD CORPORATION
International Copyright Secured   All Rights Reserved

On Top of Old Smoky

Kentucky Mountain Folksong

Strum Pattern: 8
Pick Pattern: 8

Verse
Moderately

1. On top of old smo - ky, _____ all cov - ered with snow, _____ I

2. - 8. *See additional lyrics*

lost my true lov - er, _____ by a - court-in' too slow. _____ 2. Well, a - _____

Additional Lyrics

2. Well, a-courting's a pleasure,
   And parting is grief.
   But a false-hearted lover
   Is worse than a thief.

3. A thief he will rob you
   And take all you have,
   But a false-hearted lover
   Will send you to your grave.

4. And the grave will decay you
   And turn you to dust.
   And where is the young man
   A poor girl can trust?

5. They'll hug and kiss you
   And tell you more lies
   Than the cross-ties on the railroad,
   Or the stars in the skies.

6. They'll tell you they love you,
   Just to give your heart ease.
   But the minute your back's turned,
   They'll court whom they please.

7. So come all you young maidens
   And listen to me.
   Never place your affection
   On a green willow tree.

8. For the leaves they will wither
   And the roots they will die.
   And your true love will leave you,
   And you'll never know why.

Copyright © 1996 by HAL LEONARD CORPORATION
International Copyright Secured   All Rights Reserved

The Parting Glass

Irish Folksong

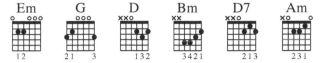

Strum Pattern: 3
Pick Pattern: 3

Verse
Moderately

1. Oh, __ all the mon - ey __ e'er I had, I __ spent it in __ good __
2., 3. *See additional lyrics*

com - pa - ny. And __ all the harm I've __ ev - er done, a - las it was __ to __

none but me. And all __ I've __ done for want __ of __ wit to

mem - 'ry now __ I __ can't re - call, so __ fill to me the __

part - ing glass, good - night and joy __ be __ with you all. 2. Oh, __ with you all.

Additional Lyrics

2. Oh, all the comrades e'er I had,
They're sorry for my going away.
And all the sweethearts e'er I had,
They'd wish me one more day to stay.
But since it falls unto my lot,
I gently rise and softly call,
That I should go and you should not,
Goodnight and joy be with you all.

3. If I had money enough to spend,
And leisure time to sit awhile,
There is a fair maid in this town
That sorely has my heart beguiled.
Her rosy cheeks and ruby lips,
I own she has my heart in thrall.
Then fill to me the parting glass,
Goodnight and joy be with you all.

Copyright © 2002 by HAL LEONARD CORPORATION
International Copyright Secured   All Rights Reserved

Pay Me My Money Down

Carribean Work Song

Strum Pattern: 5
Pick Pattern: 4

Verse
Moderately fast

1. Pay me, — oh, pay me, — pay me my mon-ey down. —
2. – 5. *See additional lyrics*

Pay me or go to jail, — pay me my mon-ey down. mon-ey down. —

Additional Lyrics

2. Thought I heard the captain say,
Pay me my money down.
'Morrow is our sailing day,
Pay me my money down.

3. Next day we cleared the bar,
Pay me my money down.
He knocked me down with the end of a spar,
Pay me my money down.

4. Wish I was Mister Howard's son,
Pay me my money down.
Sit in the house and drink all the rum.
Pay me my money down.

5. Wish I was Mister Steven's son,
Pay me my money down.
Sit in the shade and watch all the work done.
Pay me my money down.

Copyright © 2002 by HAL LEONARD CORPORATION
International Copyright Secured   All Rights Reserved

Sakura
(Cherry Blossoms)

Traditional Japanese Folksong

Strum Pattern: 4
Pick Pattern: 3

Moderately slow

Sa - ku - ra!   Sa - ku - ra!   Ya   yo - i - no   so   ra — wa
Sa - ku - ra!   Sa - ku - ra!   Cher - ry   blos - soms   fill   the — air,

mi   wa - ta - su   ka - gi - ri.   Ka - su - mi   ka   ku - mo   ka,   ni   o - i - zo
smell their   fra - grance   ev - 'ry - where.   Win - ter - time   is   fi - nal - ly past,   now   the   spring is

i - zu - ru.   I - za - ya!   I - za - ya!   Mi — ni — yu - kan.
here at — last.   Come with   me!   Come with   me!   Let   us   feel   the   sun - shine fair.

Copyright © 2002 by HAL LEONARD CORPORATION
International Copyright Secured   All Rights Reserved

The Red River Valley

Traditional American Cowboy Song

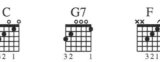

Strum Pattern: 4
Pick Pattern: 5

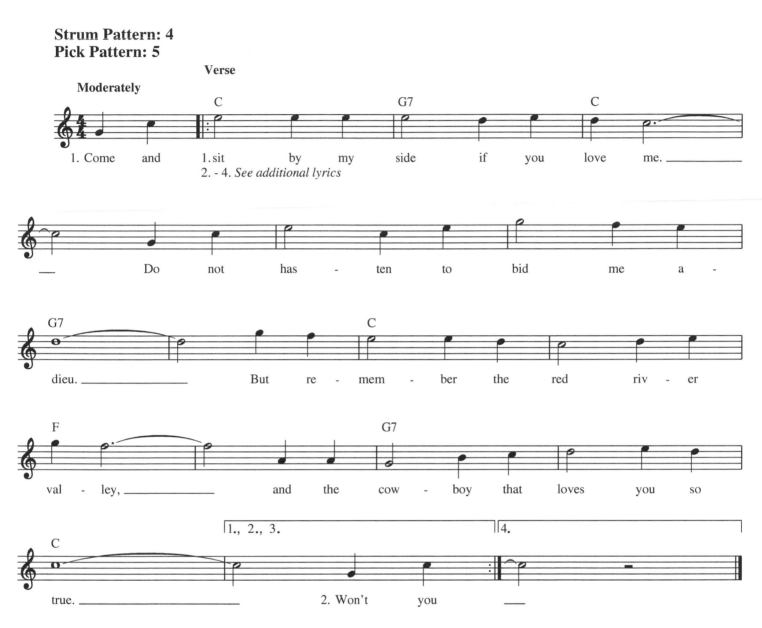

Additional Lyrics

2. Won't you think of this valley you're leaving?
   Oh, how lonely, how sad it will be.
   Oh, think of the fond heart you're breaking.
   And the grief you are causing me.

3. From this valley they say your are going.
   When you may your darling go, too?
   Would you leave her behind unprotected,
   When she loves no other but you?

4. I have promised you, darling, that never
   Will a word from my lips cause you pain.
   And my life, it will be yours forever,
   If you only will love me again.

Copyright © 1996 by HAL LEONARD CORPORATION
International Copyright Secured   All Rights Reserved

Rock-A-My Soul

African-American Spiritual

Strum Pattern: 3, 4
Pick Pattern: 4, 5

Additional Lyrics

2. When I came home from the valley at night,
   Oh, rock-a-my-soul,
   I knew that everything would be alright,
   Oh, rock-a-my-soul.

3. I felt so sad on the morning before,
   Oh, rock-a-my-soul,
   I found the peace that I was looking for,
   Oh, rock-a-my-soul.

4. The sun shines bright on the cloudiest day,
   Oh, rock-a-my-soul,
   A prayer is all you need to light your way,
   Oh, rock-a-my-soul.

Copyright © 2001 by HAL LEONARD CORPORATION
International Copyright Secured   All Rights Reserved

Sailing, Sailing

Words and Music by Godfrey Marks

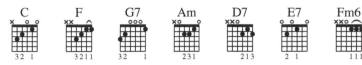

Strum Pattern: 8
Pick Pattern: 8

Sail - ing, sail - ing o - ver the bound - ing main. _____ For

man - y a storm - y wind shall blow, ere Jack ___ comes home a - gain.

Sail - ing, sail - ing, o - ver the bound - ing main. _____ For

man - y a storm - y wind shall blow, ere Jack comes home a - gain. ___

Copyright © 1998 by HAL LEONARD CORPORATION
International Copyright Secured   All Rights Reserved

Saint James Infirmary

Words and Music by Joe Primrose

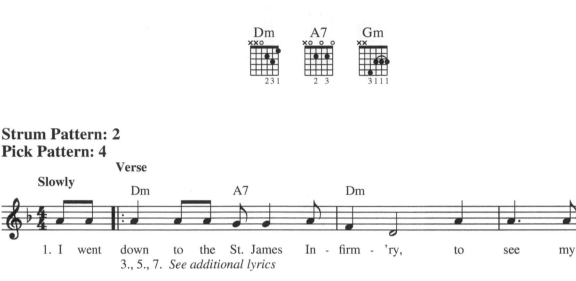

Strum Pattern: 2
Pick Pattern: 4

1. I went down to the St. James In - firm - 'ry, to see my ba - by
3., 5., 7. *See additional lyrics*

there. She was ly - in' on a long white ta - ble, so ___

sweet, so ___ cool, ___ so fair. 2. Went up to see the doc - tor, "She's
4., 6., 8. *See additional lyrics*

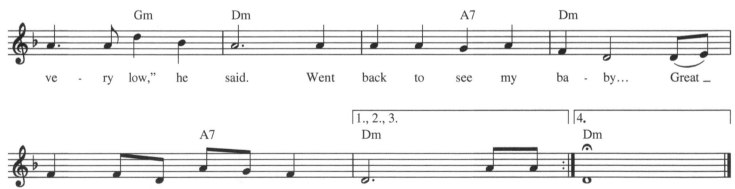

ve - ry low," he said. Went back to see my ba - by... Great ___

God! She was ly - in' there dead. 3. I went blues.

Additional Lyrics

3. I went down to old Joe's barroom,
On the corner by the square.
They were servin' the drinks as usual,
And the usual crowd was there.

4. On my left stood Joe McKennedy;
His eyes bloodshot red.
He turned to the crowd around him,
These are the words he said:

5. Let her go, let her go, God bless her;
Wherever she may be.
She may search this wide world over;
She'll never find a man like me.

6. Oh, when I die, please bury me
In my high-top Stetson hat;
Put a gold piece on my watch chain
So they'll know I died standin' pat.

7. Get six gamblers to carry my coffin,
Six chorus girls to sing my song.
Put a jazz band on my tail gate
To raise hell as we go along.

8. Now that's the end of my story;
Let's have another round of booze;
And if anyone should ask you, just tell them
I've got the St. James Infirmary blues.

Copyright © 2002 by HAL LEONARD CORPORATION
International Copyright Secured   All Rights Reserved

Santa Lucia

By Teodoro Cottrau

Strum Pattern: 8, 9
Pick Pattern: 8, 9

Verse
Slowly

1. Now 'neath the sil - ver moon, o - cean is glow - ing.
2., 3., 4. *See additional lyrics*

O'er the calm bil - lows, soft winds are blow - ing. Hark, how the

sail - ors cry, joy - ous - ly ech - oes sigh, San - ta __ Lu - ci - a,

D.C. al Coda
(take repeat)

San - ta Lu - ci - a.

Coda

San - ta Lu - ci - a.

Additional Lyrics

2. Here balmy breezes blow, pure joys invite us.
   And as we gently row, all things delight us.

3. When o'er the waters, light winds are playing;
   Their spell can soothe us, all care allaying.

4. Thee, sweet Napoli, what charms are given.
   Where smiles creation, toil blessed heaven.

Copyright © 2002 by HAL LEONARD CORPORATION
International Copyright Secured All Rights Reserved

Scarborough Fair

Traditional English

Strum Pattern: 7
Pick Pattern: 7

Verse
Gently

1. Are you go - ing to Scar - bor-ough Fair? Pars - ley, sage, rose -
2. – 8. *See additional lyrics*

ma - ry and thyme. Re - mem - ber me to one who lives there, _ for

once she was a true love of mine. _____ mine. _____

Additional Lyrics

2. Tell her to make me a cambric shirt,
   Parsley, sage, rosemary and thyme,
   Without any seam or fine needlework,
   For once she was a true love of mine.

3. Tell her to wash it in yonder dry well,
   Parsley, sage, rosemary and thyme,
   Where water ne'er spring, nor drop of rain fell,
   For once she was a true love of mine.

4. Tell her to dry in on yonder thorn,
   Parsley, sage, rosemary and thyme,
   Which never bore blossom since Adam was born,
   For once she was a true love of mine.

5. Will you find me an acre of land,
   Parsley, sage, rosemary and thyme,
   Between the sea foam and the sea sand,
   For once she was a true love of mine.

6. Will you plough it with a lamb's horn,
   Parsley, sage, rosemary and thyme,
   And sow it all over with one peppercorn,
   For once she was a true love of mine.

7. Will you reap it with sickle of leather,
   Parsley, sage, rosemary and thyme,
   And tie it all up with a peacock's feather,
   For once she was a true love of mine.

8. When you're done and finished your work,
   Parsley, sage, rosemary and thyme,
   Then come to me for your cambric shirt,
   And you shall be a true love of mine.

Copyright © 2002 by HAL LEONARD CORPORATION
International Copyright Secured   All Rights Reserved

Shalom Chaveyrim
(Shalom Friends)

Traditional Hebrew Singalong

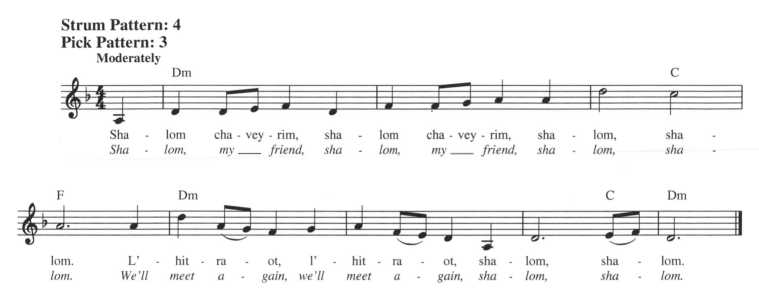

Strum Pattern: 4
Pick Pattern: 3

Sha - lom cha - vey - rim, sha - lom cha - vey - rim, sha - lom, sha -
Sha - lom, my ___ friend, sha - lom, my ___ friend, sha - lom, ___ sha -

lom. L' - hit - ra - ot, l' - hit - ra - ot, sha - lom, sha - lom.
lom. We'll meet a - gain, we'll meet a - gain, sha - lom, sha - lom.

Copyright © 2002 by HAL LEONARD CORPORATION
International Copyright Secured   All Rights Reserved

Shenandoah

American Folksong

Strum Pattern: 1
Pick Pattern: 2

O Shen - an - doah, ___ I love to see you. A -

way, ___ you roll - ing riv - er. O Shen-an-doah, ___ I long to see you. A -

way, ___ I'm bond a - way ___ a - cross the wide ___ Mis - sour - i.

Copyright © 1996 by HAL LEONARD CORPORATION
International Copyright Secured   All Rights Reserved

She'll Be Comin' 'Round the Mountain

Traditional

Strum Pattern: 2
Pick Pattern: 4

1. She'll be com-in' 'round the moun-tain when she comes.
2. - 4. *See additional lyrics*

She'll be com-in' round the moun-tain when she comes.

She'll be com-in' 'round the moun-tain, she'll be

com-in' 'round the moun-tain, she'll be com-in' 'round the

moun-tain when she comes. _____ 2. She'll be _____

Additional Lyrics

2. She'll be drivin' six white horses when she comes.
She'll be drivin' six white horses when she comes.
She'll be drivin' six white horses,
She'll be drivin' six white horses,
She'll be drivin' six white horses when she comes.

3. Oh, we'll all go out to meet her when she comes.
Oh, we'll all go out to meet her when she comes.
Oh, we'll all go out to meet her,
Oh, we'll all go out to meet her,
Yes, we'll all go out to meet her when she comes.

4. She'll be wearin' a blue bonnet when she comes.
She'll be wearin' a blue bonnet when she comes.
She'll be wearin' a blue bonnet,
She'll be wearin' a blue bonnet,
She'll be wearin' a blue bonnet when she comes.

Copyright © 1996 by HAL LEONARD CORPORATION
International Copyright Secured   All Rights Reserved

Simple Gifts

Traditional Shaker Hymn

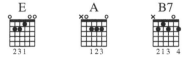

Copyright © 1996 by HAL LEONARD CORPORATION
International Copyright Secured   All Rights Reserved

Sinner Man

Traditional

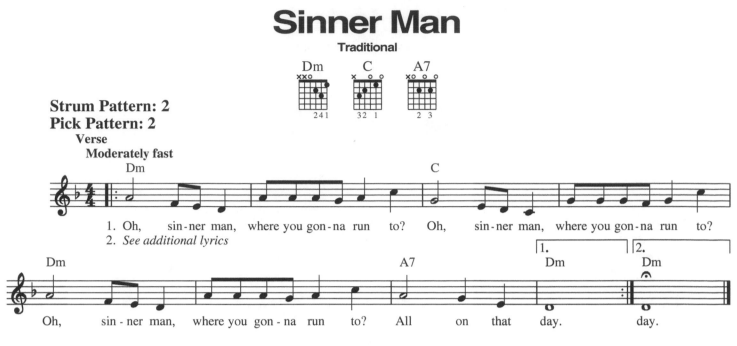

Strum Pattern: 2
Pick Pattern: 2

Verse
Moderately fast

1. Oh, sin-ner man, where you gon-na run to? Oh, sin-ner man, where you gon-na run to?
2. *See additional lyrics*

Oh, sin-ner man, where you gon-na run to? All on that day. day.

Additional Lyrics

2. Run to the rock, rock won't you hide me?
Run to the rock, rock won't you hide me?
Run to the rock, rock won't you hide me?
All on that day.

Copyright © 2002 by HAL LEONARD CORPORATION
International Copyright Secured   All Rights Reserved

Sometimes I Feel Like a Motherless Child

African-American Spiritual

Strum Pattern: 10
Pick Pattern: 10

Verse
Slowly

1. Some-times I feel like a moth-er-less child. ___ Some-times I
2. Some-times I feel like I'm al-most gone. ___ Some-times I

feel like a moth-er-less child. ___ Some-times I feel like a
feel llike I'm al-most gone. ___ Some-times I feel like I'm

moth-er-less child, ___ a long way ___ from home, ___
al-most gone, ___ a long ways ___ from home. ___

Copyright © 1996 by HAL LEONARD CORPORATION
International Copyright Secured   All Rights Reserved

Song of the Volga Boatman

Russian Folksong

Strum Pattern: 4
Pick Pattern: 3

Copyright © 2002 by HAL LEONARD CORPORATION
International Copyright Secured All Rights Reserved

Streets of Laredo

American Cowboy Song

Strum Pattern: 8
Pick Pattern: 8

Verse
Moderately

1. As I ____ walked out in the streets of La - re - do, as I walked
see by your out - fit that you are a cow - boy." These words, he did

out in La - re - do one day, I spied a young cow - boy all wrapped up in
say as I proud - ly stopped by. "Come sit down be - side me and hear my sad

lin - en, wrapped in white lin - en as cold as the day. 2. "I
stor - y. Got shot in the breast and I know I must die."

Copyright © 1996 by HAL LEONARD CORPORATION
International Copyright Secured   All Rights Reserved

Sweet Rosie O'Grady

Words and Music by Maude Nugent

Strum Pattern: 3
Pick Pattern: 4

Verse
Moderately

1. Just down a - round the cor - ner of the street where I re - side, there lives the cut - est lit - tle girl that
2. *See additional lyrics*

I have ev - er spied. Her name is Rose O' Gra - dy and, I don't mind tell - ing you, that

Copyright © 2002 by HAL LEONARD CORPORATION
International Copyright Secured   All Rights Reserved

Strum Pattern: 7
Pick Pattern: 8

Additional Lyrics

2. I never shall forget the day she promised to be mine,
   As we sat telling love tales in the golden summertime.
   'Twas on her finger that I placed a small engagement ring,
   While in the trees, the little birds this song they seemed to sing:

Sweet Betsy from Pike

American Folksong

Strum Pattern: 7
Pick Pattern: 9

Verse

Brightly

1. Did you ev - er hear tell of sweet Bet - sy from Pike, who
2., 3. *See additional lyrics*

crossed the wide prai - ries with her lov - er Ike? With two yoke of

ox - en and one spot - ted hog, a ___ tall shag - hai roost - er, an

Chorus

old yel - low dog. Sing, ___ "Too - ral - i, oo - ral - i, oo - ral - i -

ay." Sing, ___ "Too - ral - i, oo - ral - i, oo - ral - i - ay." 2. One ___ ay."

Additional Lyrics

2. One evening quite early the camped on the Platte,
   'Twas near by the road on a green shady flat
   Where Betsy, quite tired, lay down to repose
   While with wonder Ike gazed on his Pike County rose.

3. They stopped at Salt Lake to inquire the way,
   Where Brigham declared that sweet Bets should stay.
   But Betsy got frightened and ran like a deer,
   While Brigham stood pawing the ground like a steer.

Copyright © 1996 by HAL LEONARD CORPORATION
International Copyright Secured   All Rights Reserved

Swing Low, Sweet Chariot

Traditional Spiritual

Strum Pattern: 2
Pick Pattern: 4

Chorus
Moderately

Swing low, sweet char - i - ot, ___ com - in' for to car - ry me home. Swing low, sweet char - i - ot, ___ com - in' for to car - ry me home. 1. I

Verse

look o - ver Jor - dan, and what do I see, ___ com - in' for to car - ry me
2. *See additional lyrics*

home? A band ___ of an - gels com - in' af - ter me, ___

com - in' for to car - ry me home. home. home.

Additional Lyrics

2. If you get there before I do,
   Coming for to carry me home,
   Tell all my friends I'm coming too,
   Coming for to carry me home.

Copyright © 2001 by HAL LEONARD CORPORATION
International Copyright Secured   All Rights Reserved

This Little Light of Mine

African-American Spiritual

Strum Pattern: 2
Pick Pattern: 4

Copyright © 1996 by HAL LEONARD CORPORATION
International Copyright Secured   All Rights Reserved

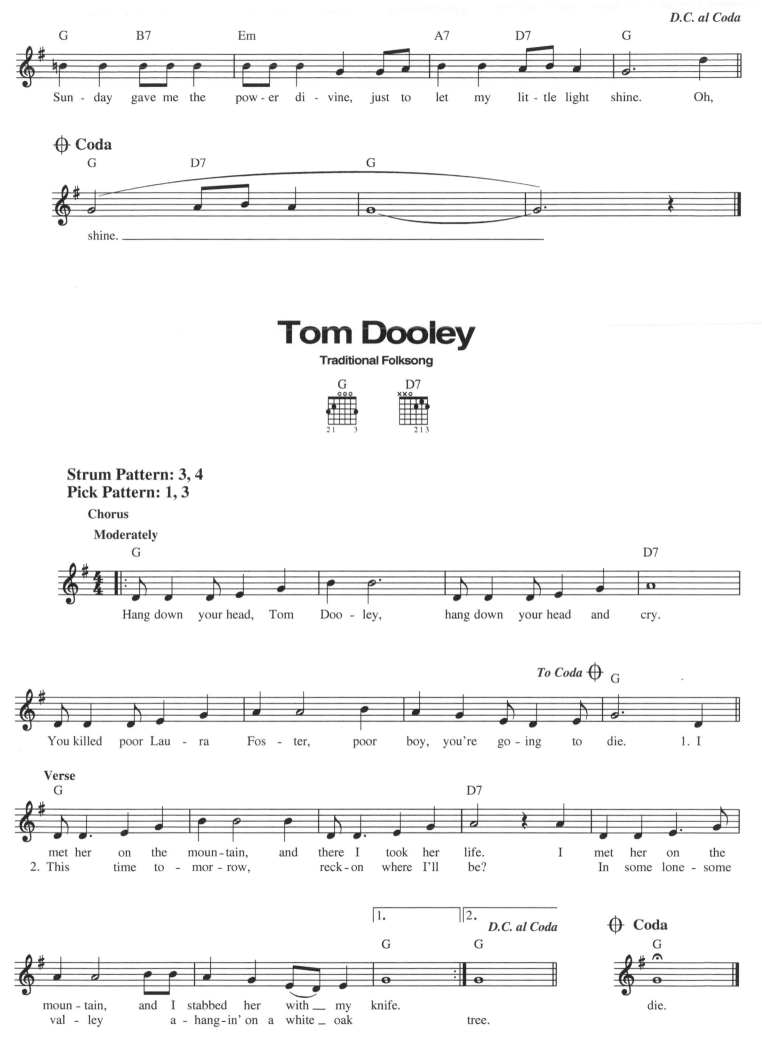

Tom Dooley

Traditional Folksong

Strum Pattern: 3, 4
Pick Pattern: 1, 3

Chorus

Moderately

Hang down your head, Tom Doo - ley, hang down your head and cry.

You killed poor Lau - ra Fos - ter, poor boy, you're go - ing to die. 1. I

Verse

met her on the moun - tain, and there I took her life. I met her on the
2. This time to - mor - row, reck - on where I'll be? In some lone - some

1. moun - tain, and I stabbed her with my knife.
2. val - ley a - hang - in' on a white oak tree.

D.C. al Coda

Coda

die.

Copyright © 2001 by HAL LEONARD CORPORATION
International Copyright Secured   All Rights Reserved

This Old Man

Traditional

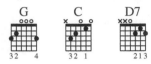

Strum Pattern: 3
Pick Pattern: 3

Verse
Lively

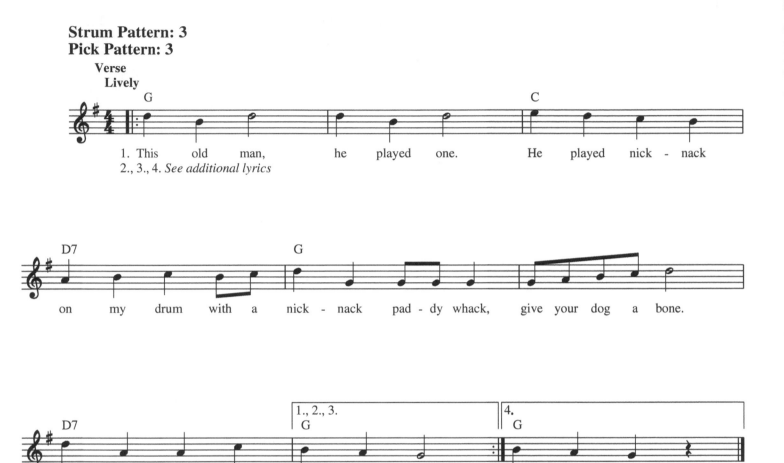

1. This old man, he played one. He played nick-nack
2., 3., 4. *See additional lyrics*

on my drum with a nick-nack pad-dy whack, give your dog a bone.

This old man came roll-ing home. roll-ing home.

Additional Lyrics

2. This old man, he played two.
He played nicknack on my shoe with a
Nicknack paddy whack, give your dog a bone.
This old man came rolling home.

3. This old man, he played three.
He played nicknack on my knee with a
Nicknack paddy whack, give your dog a bone.
This old man came rolling home.

4. This old man, he played four.
He played nicknack on my door with a
Nicknack paddy whack, give your dog a bone.
This old man came rolling home.

Copyright © 1998 by HAL LEONARD CORPORATION
International Copyright Secured   All Rights Reserved

This Train

Traditional

Strum Pattern: 2
Pick Pattern: 4

Verse
With Spirit

1. This train is bound for glo-ry, this train._____
2. - 6. *See additional lyrics*

This train is bound for glo-ry, this train._____

This train is bound for glo-ry, don't ride noth-in' but the

Chorus

right-eous and the ho-ly. This train is bound for glo-ry,

1. - 5.

this train._____

6.

this train._____

Additional Lyrics

2. This train don't carry no gamblers, this train.
   This train don't carry no gamblers, this train.
   This train don't carry no gamblers,
   No hypocrites, no midnight ramblers.

3. This train don't carry no liars, this train.
   This train don't carry no liars, this train.
   This train don't carry no liars,
   No hypocrites and no high flyers.

4. This train is built for speed now, this train.
   This train is built for speed now, this train.
   This train is built for speed now,
   Fastest train you ever did see.

5. This train you don't pay no transportation, this train.
   This train you don't pay no transportation, this train.
   This train you don't pay no transportation,
   No Jim Crow and no discrimination.

6. This train don't carry no rustlers, this train.
   This train don't carry no rustlers, this train.
   This train don't carry no rustlers,
   Sidestreet walkers, two-bit hustlers.

Copyright © 1998 by HAL LEONARD CORPORATION
International Copyright Secured   All Rights Reserved

Too-Ra-Loo-Ra-Loo-Ral
(That's an Irish Lullaby)
from GOING MY WAY

Words and Music by James R. Shannon

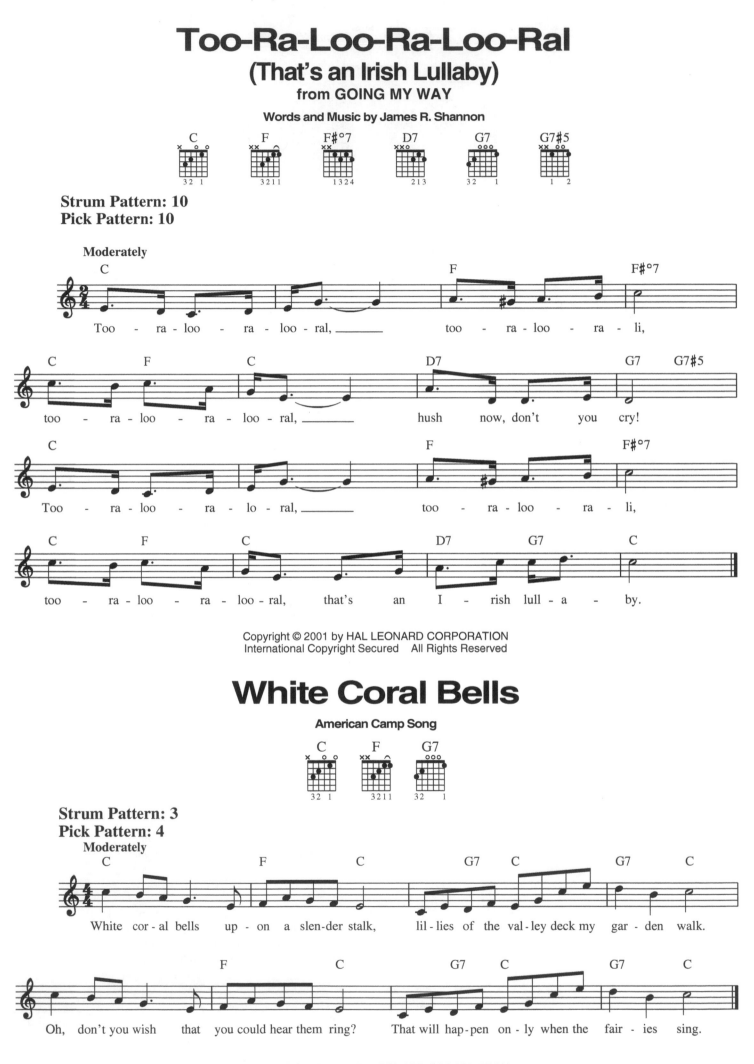

Strum Pattern: 10
Pick Pattern: 10

Copyright © 2001 by HAL LEONARD CORPORATION
International Copyright Secured   All Rights Reserved

White Coral Bells

American Camp Song

Strum Pattern: 3
Pick Pattern: 4

Copyright © 2002 by HAL LEONARD CORPORATION
International Copyright Secured   All Rights Reserved

Tramp! Tramp! Tramp!

Words and Music by George F. Root

Strum Pattern: 3
Pick Pattern: 3

Verse

Moderately

1. In the pris - on cell I sit, think - ing, moth - er dear, of you, and our
2., 3. *See additional lyrics*

bright and hap - py home so far a - way; and the tears they fill my eyes, spite of

all that I can do, though I try to cheer my com - rades and be gay.

Chorus

Tramp! Tramp! Tramp! the boys are march - ing. Cheer up, com - rades, they will

come, and be - neath the star - ry flag we shall breathe the air a - gain of the

free land in our own be - lov - ed home. 2. In the home.

Additional Lyrics

2. In the battle front we stood when their fiercest charge they made,
   And they swept us off a hundred men or more;
   But before we reached their lines, they were beaten back, dismayed,
   And we heard the cry of vict'ry o'er and o'er.

3. So, within the prison cell, we are waiting for the day
   That shall come to open wide the iron door,
   And the hollow eye grows bright, and the poor heart almost gay,
   As we think of seeing home and friends once more.

Copyright © 2002 by HAL LEONARD CORPORATION
International Copyright Secured   All Rights Reserved

Tum Balalaika
(Play the Balalaika)

Yiddish Folksong

Am   E   E7   Dm   F   G7   C

Strum Pattern: 7
Pick Pattern: 9

Verse
Moderately

Am

1. Shteyt   a   boch - er   un _____ er   tracht,   tracht   und   tracht   di
1. *A   young   man   is   deep _____ in   thought,   and   he   won - ders*
2., 3. *See additional lyrics*

Am   Dm   Am   Dm

gan - tze   nacht   ve - men   tsu   ne - men,   un   nit   far - she - men,   ve - men,   tsu
whom _ he   ought   to   take   as   wife   for   all   of   his   life,   to   take _ as

Chorus

E   E7   Am   Am   E7

ne - men,   un   nit   far   she - men.   Tum   ba - la,   tum   ba - la,   tum   ba - la - lai - ka,
wife   for   all   of   his   life. _____

Am   F   G7

tum   ba - la,   tum   ba - la,   tum   ba - la - lai - ka,   tum - ba - la - lai - ka.   Shpil   ba - la -
Play   ba - la -

C   Dm   E7 |1., 2. |3.
                                              Am   Am

lai - ka,   tum   ba - la - lai - ka,   frey - lich   zol   zayn.   zayn.
lai - ka,   play   ba - la - lai - ka,   let   there   be   joy.   joy.

Additional Lyrics

Yiddish

2. Meydl, meydl, ich vil bay der fregn,
   Vos ken vaksn, vaksn on regn?
   Vos ken brenen un nit oyfheren,
   Vos ken beynken, veynen on treren.

3. Narisher bocher, vos darfst du fregn,
   A shteyn ken vaksn, vaksn on regn.
   A libe ken brenen un nit oyfheren,
   A hartz ken beynken, veynen on treren.

English

2. Tell me, maiden, I'd like to know,
   What it is needs no rain to grow?
   What's not consumed, although it's burning,
   What weeps no tears, although it's yearning?

3. You foolish boy didn't you know,
   A stone does not need rain to grow?
   A love's not consumed, although it's burning,
   A heart weeps no tears, although it's yearning.

Copyright © 2002 by HAL LEONARD CORPORATION
International Copyright Secured   All Rights Reserved

Vicar of Bray

Traditional

Strum Pattern: 4
Pick Pattern: 3

Verse
Moderately

1. In good King Charles' gold-en days, when loy-al-ty no harm meant, a
2. – 5. *See additional lyrics*

zeal-ous high church-man I was, and so I gain'd pre-fer-ment. To teach my flock I

nev-er miss'd: Kings are by God ap-poin-ted, and damned are those who dare re-sist, or

Chorus

touch the Lord's a-noin-ted. And this is law, I will main-tain, un-til my dy-ing

1. – 4. *5.*

day, sir, that what-so-ev-er king shall reign, I'll still be the Vi-car of Bray, sir! 2. When Bray, sir!

Additional Lyrics

2. When royal James obtained the crown
   And pop'ry came in fashion,
   The penal laws I hooted down
   And read the declaration.
   The church of Rome I found would fit
   Full well my constitution,
   And I had been a Jesuit
   But for the revolution.

3. When William was our king declar'd
   To heal the nation's grievance,
   With this new wind about I steer'd
   And swore to him allegiance.
   Old principles I did revoke,
   Set conscience at a distance,
   Passive resistance was a joke,
   A jest was nonresistance.

4. When George in pudding time came o'er,
   And mod'rate men look'd big, sir,
   I turn'd the "cat in pan" once more,
   And so became a Whig, sir.
   And this preferment I procured
   From our new faith's defender,
   And almost ev'ry day abjured
   The Pope and the Pretender.

5. The illustrious Houses of Hanover
   And Protestant succession,
   To these I lustily will swear
   While they can keep possession.
   For in my faith and loyalty
   I never once will falter,
   And George my lawful King shall be,
   Except the times should alter.

Copyright © 2002 by HAL LEONARD CORPORATION
International Copyright Secured All Rights Reserved

Vive L'amour

Traditional

Strum Pattern: 7, 8
Pick Pattern: 7, 8

Verse
Moderately

1. Let ev - 'ry good fel - low now fill up his glass,
2. *See additional lyrics*

Vi - ve la com - pag - nie, _____ and drink to the health of our

glo - ri - ous class, Vi - ve la com - pag - nie.

Chorus

Vi - ve la, vi - ve la, vi - ve l'a - mour, vi - ve la, vi - ve la,

vi - ve l'a - mour, vi - ve l'a - mour, vi - ve l'a - mour,

1.
vi - ve la com - pag - nie! _____
2.
2. Let ___

Additional Lyrics

2. Let every married man drink to his wife,
   Viva la compagnie.
   The joy of his bosom and plague of his life,
   Viva la compagnie.

Copyright © 2001 by HAL LEONARD CORPORATION
International Copyright Secured   All Rights Reserved

The Wabash Cannon Ball

Hobo Song

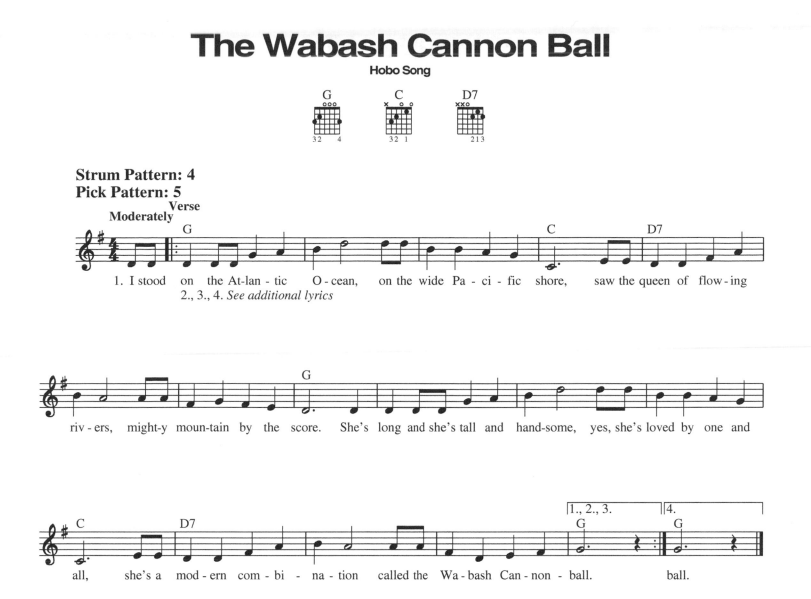

Strum Pattern: 4
Pick Pattern: 5

1. I stood on the At-lan-tic O-cean, on the wide Pa-ci-fic shore, saw the queen of flow-ing
2., 3., 4. *See additional lyrics*

riv-ers, might-y moun-tain by the score. She's long and she's tall and hand-some, yes, she's loved by one and

all, she's a mod-ern com-bi-na-tion called the Wa-bash Can-non-ball. ball.

Additional Lyrics

2. Listen to the jingle, the rumble and the roar,
   Riding through the woodlands, to the hills and by the shore.
   Hear the mighty rush of the engine, hear the lonesome hobo squall,
   Riding through the jungle on the Wabash Cannonball.

3. Eastern states are dandies so the Western people say,
   From New York to St. Louis and Chicago by the way.
   Through the hills of Minnesota where the rippling waters fall,
   No chances can be taken on the Wabash Cannonball.

4. Here's to Daddy Claxton, may his name forever stand.
   May he ever be remembered through the parts of all our land.
   When his earthly race is over and the curtain 'round him fall,
   We'll carry him to glory on the Wabash Cannonball.

Copyright © 1996 by HAL LEONARD CORPORATION
International Copyright Secured   All Rights Reserved

Water Is Wide

Traditional

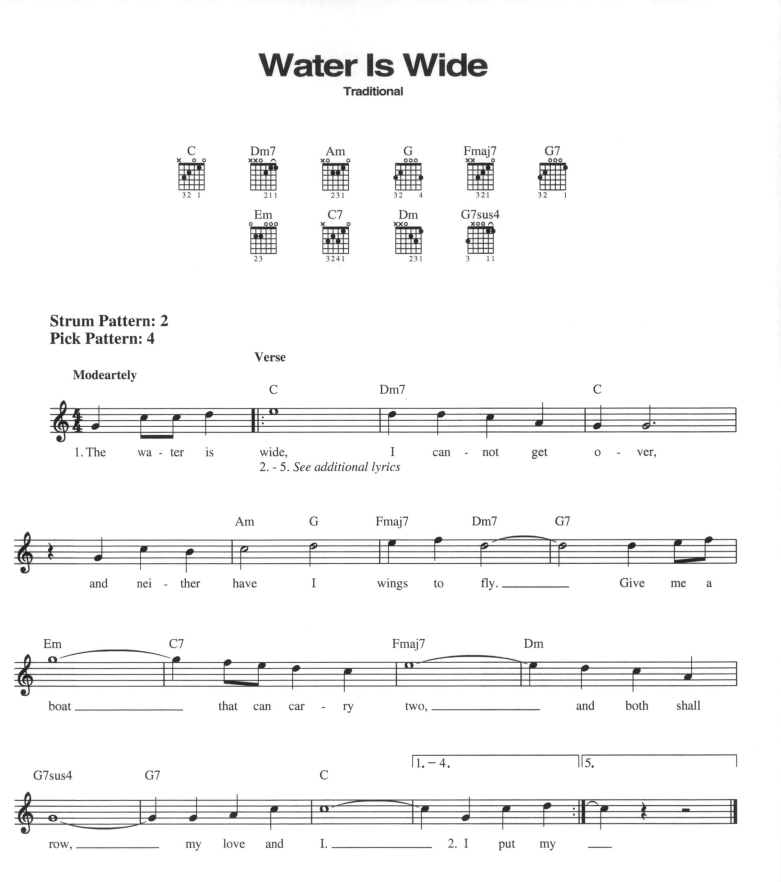

Strum Pattern: 2
Pick Pattern: 4

Additional Lyrics

2. I put my hand into some soft bush,
   Thinking the sweetest flower to find.
   The thorn, it stuck me to the bone,
   And oh, I left that flower alone.

3. A ship there is and she sails the sea,
   She's loaded deep as deep can be.
   But not so deep as the love I'm in,
   And I know not how to sink or swim.

4. Oh, love is handsome and love is fine,
   Gay as a jewel when first it's new.
   But love grows old and waxes cold,
   And fades away like summer dew.

5. I leaned my back against a young oak,
   Thinking he was a trusty tree.
   But first he bended and then he broke,
   And thus did my false love to me.

Copyright © 1996 by HAL LEONARD CORPORATION
International Copyright Secured   All Rights Reserved

Wayfaring Stranger

Southern American Folk Hymn

Strum Pattern: 3
Pick Pattern: 4

Additional Lyrics

2. I know dark clouds will gather round me,
   I know my way is rough and steep;
   But golden fields lie out before me
   Where God's redeemed shall ever sleep.
   I'm going there to see my mother
   She said she'd meet me when I come.
   I'm only going over Jordan,
   I'm only going over home.

3. I'll soon be free from ev'ry trial,
   My body sleep in the church yard;
   I'll drop the cross of self denial
   And enter on my great reward.
   I'm going there to see my Savior
   To sing His praise forever more.
   I'm only going over Jordan,
   I'm only going over home.

Copyright © 2001 by HAL LEONARD CORPORATION
International Copyright Secured   All Rights Reserved

When Irish Eyes Are Smiling

Words by Chauncey Olcott and George Graff, Jr.
Music by Ernest R. Ball

Strum Pattern: 7, 9
Pick Pattern: 8

Copyright © 2001 by HAL LEONARD CORPORATION
International Copyright Secured   All Rights Reserved

When the Saints Go Marching In

Words by Katherine E. Purvis
Music by James M. Black

Strum Pattern: 1
Pick Pattern: 2

Additional Lyrics

2. Oh, when the sun refuse to shine,
Oh, when the sun refuse to shine,
Oh Lord, I want to be in that number,
When the sun refuse to shine.

3. Oh, when they crown Him Lord of all,
Oh, when they crown Him Lord of all,
Oh Lord, I want to be in that number,
When they crown Him Lord of all.

4. Oh, when they gather 'round the throne,
Oh, when they gather 'round the throne,
Oh Lord, I want to be in that number,
When they gather 'round the throne.

Copyright © 1998 by HAL LEONARD CORPORATION
International Copyright Secured   All Rights Reserved

Wildwood Flower

Traditional

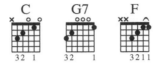

Strum Pattern: 3
Pick Pattern: 4

1. I will twine and will min-gle my wav-ing black hair with the ros-es so red and the
2. – 5. *See additional lyrics*

lil-y so fair, the myr-tle so green of an em-er-ald hue, the

pale am-a-ni-ta and its lip so blue. 2. Oh, he frail wild-wood flower.

Additional Lyrics

2. Oh, he promised to love me,
   He promised to love,
   And to cherish me always
   All others above.
   I woke from my dream
   And my idol was clay.
   My passion for loving
   Had vanished away.

3. I'll dance and I'll sing
   And my life shall be gay,
   I'll charm every heart
   In the crowd I survey;
   Though my heart now is breaking,
   He never shall know
   How his name makes me tremble,
   My pale cheeks to glow.

4. Oh, he taught me to love him,
   He called me his flower,
   A blossom to cheer him
   Through life's weary hour.
   But now he is gone
   And left me alone,
   The wild flowers to weep
   And the wild birds to mourn.

5. I'll dance and I'll sing
   And my heart will be gay,
   I'll banish this weeping
   Drive troubles away.
   I'll live yet to see him
   Regret this dark hour,
   When he won and neglected
   This frail wildwood flower.

Copyright © 2002 by HAL LEONARD CORPORATION
International Copyright Secured   All Rights Reserved

Worried Man Blues

Traditional

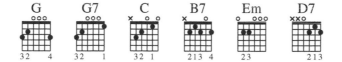

Strum Pattern: 3
Pick Pattern: 1

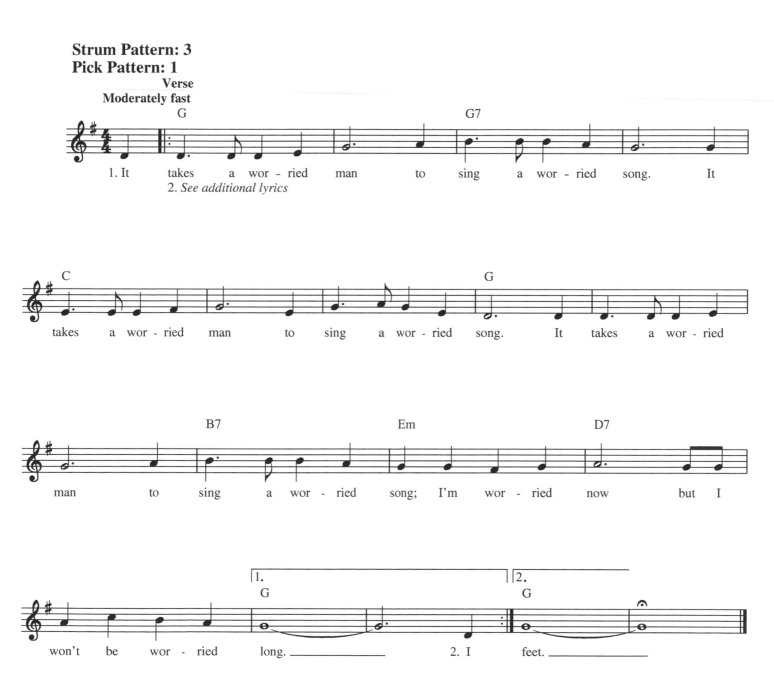

Verse
Moderately fast

1. It takes a wor-ried man to sing a wor-ried song. It
2. *See additional lyrics*

takes a wor-ried man to sing a wor-ried song. It takes a wor-ried

man to sing a wor-ried song; I'm wor-ried now but I

won't be wor-ried long. _____ 2. I feet. _____

Additional Lyrics

2. I went across the river and I lay down to sleep.
   I went across the river and I lay down to sleep.
   I went across the river and I lay down to sleep;
   When I woke up, had shackles on my feet.

Copyright © 2002 by HAL LEONARD CORPORATION
International Copyright Secured   All Rights Reserved

Yankee Doodle

Traditional

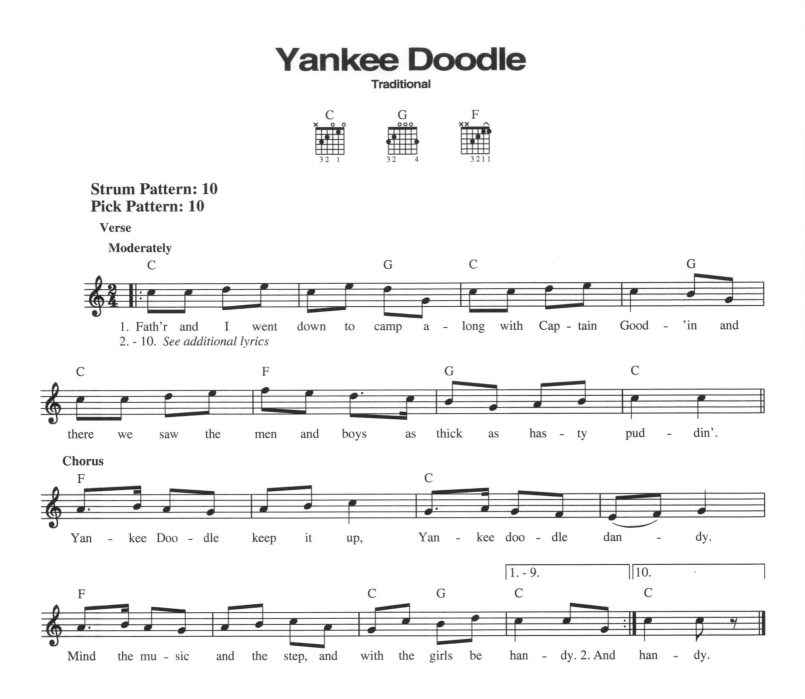

Strum Pattern: 10
Pick Pattern: 10

Verse

Moderately

1. Fath'r and I went down to camp a - long with Cap - tain Good - 'in and
2. - 10. *See additional lyrics*

there we saw the men and boys as thick as has - ty pud - din'.

Chorus

Yan - kee Doo - dle keep it up, Yan - kee doo - dle dan - dy.

1. - 9. **10.**

Mind the mu - sic and the step, and with the girls be han - dy. 2. And han - dy.

Additional Lyrics

2. And there we see a thousand men
   As rich as Squire David.
   And what they wasted ev'ry day
   I wish it could be saved.

3. And there was Captain Washington
   Upon a slapping stallion
   A-giving orders to his men,
   I guess there was a million.

4. And then the feathers on his hat,
   They looked so very fine, ah!
   I wanted peskily to get
   To give for my Jemima.

5. And there I see a swamping gun,
   Large as a log of maple.
   Upon a mighty little cart,
   A load for father's cattle.

6. And ev'ry time they fired it off,
   It took a horn of powder.
   It made a noise like father's gun,
   Only a nation louder.

7. An' there I see a little keg,
   Its head all made of leather.
   They knocked upon't with little sticks
   To call the folks together.

8. And Cap'n Davis had a gun,
   He kind o'clapt his hand on't
   And stuck a crooked stabbing-iron
   Upon the little end on't.

9. The troopers, too, would gallop up
   And fire right in our faces.
   It scared me almost half to death
   To see them run such races.

10. It scared me so I hooked it off
    Nor stopped, as I remember.
    Nor turned about till I got home,
    Locked up in mother's chamber.

Copyright © 2002 by HAL LEONARD CORPORATION
International Copyright Secured   All Rights Reserved

THE BOOK SERIES
FOR EASY GUITAR

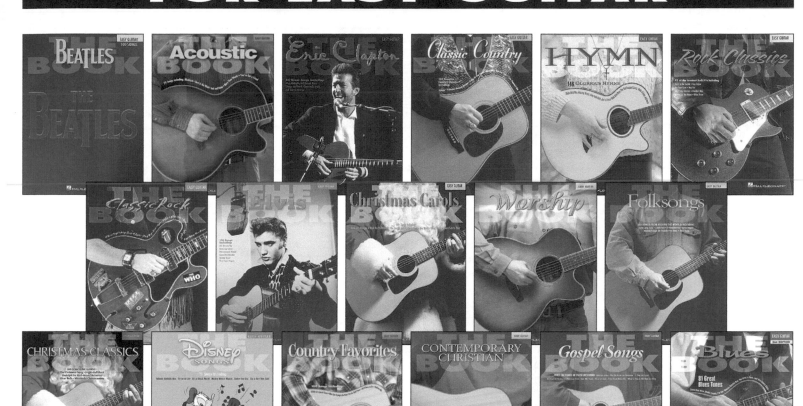

THE ACOUSTIC BOOK
00702251 Easy Guitar.....................................$16.99

THE BEATLES BOOK
00699266 Easy Guitar.....................................$19.95

THE BLUES BOOK – 2ND ED.
00702104 Easy Guitar.....................................$16.95

THE CHRISTMAS CAROLS BOOK
00702186 Easy Guitar.....................................$14.95

THE CHRISTMAS CLASSICS BOOK
00702200 Easy Guitar.....................................$14.95

THE ERIC CLAPTON BOOK
00702056 Easy Guitar.....................................$18.95

THE CLASSIC COUNTRY BOOK
00702018 Easy Guitar.....................................$19.99

THE CLASSIC ROCK BOOK
00698977 Easy Guitar.....................................$19.95

THE CONTEMPORARY CHRISTIAN BOOK
00702195 Easy Guitar.....................................$17.99

THE COUNTRY CLASSIC FAVORITES BOOK
00702238 Easy Guitar.....................................$19.99

HAL•LEONARD®
www.halleonard.com

Prices, contents, and availability
subject to change without notice.

Disney characters and artwork © Disney Enterprises, Inc.

THE DISNEY SONGS BOOK
00702168 Easy Guitar.....................................$19.95

THE FOLKSONGS BOOK
00702180 Easy Guitar.....................................$15.99

THE GOSPEL SONGS BOOK
00702157 Easy Guitar.....................................$16.99

THE HYMN BOOK
00702142 Easy Guitar.....................................$14.99

THE ELVIS BOOK
00702163 Easy Guitar.....................................$19.95

THE ROCK CLASSICS BOOK
00702055 Easy Guitar.....................................$19.99

THE WORSHIP BOOK
00702247 Easy Guitar.....................................$15.99

0717

EASY GUITAR WITH NOTES & TAB

This series features simplified arrangements with notes, tab, chord charts, and strum and pick patterns.

MIXED FOLIOS

00702287	Acoustic	$19.99
00702002	Acoustic Rock Hits for Easy Guitar	$15.99
00702166	All-Time Best Guitar Collection	$19.99
00702232	Best Acoustic Songs for Easy Guitar	$16.99
00119835	Best Children's Songs	$16.99
00703055	The Big Book of Nursery Rhymes & Children's Songs	$16.99
00698978	Big Christmas Collection	$19.99
00702394	Bluegrass Songs for Easy Guitar	$15.99
00289632	Bohemian Rhapsody	$19.99
00703387	Celtic Classics	$16.99
00224808	Chart Hits of 2016-2017	$14.99
00267383	Chart Hits of 2017-2018	$14.99
00334293	Chart Hits of 2019-2020	$16.99
00403479	Chart Hits of 2021-2022	$16.99
00702149	Children's Christian Songbook	$9.99
00702028	Christmas Classics	$8.99
00101779	Christmas Guitar	$14.99
00702141	Classic Rock	$8.95
00159642	Classical Melodies	$12.99
00253933	Disney/Pixar's Coco	$16.99
00702203	CMT's 100 Greatest Country Songs	$34.99
00702283	The Contemporary Christian Collection	$16.99

00196954	Contemporary Disney	$19.99
00702239	Country Classics for Easy Guitar	$24.99
00702257	Easy Acoustic Guitar Songs	$17.99
00702041	Favorite Hymns for Easy Guitar	$12.99
00222701	Folk Pop Songs	$17.99
00126894	Frozen	$14.99
00333922	Frozen 2	$14.99
00702286	Glee	$16.99
00702160	The Great American Country Songbook	$19.99
00702148	Great American Gospel for Guitar	$14.99
00702050	Great Classical Themes for Easy Guitar	$9.99
00275088	The Greatest Showman	$17.99
00148030	Halloween Guitar Songs	$14.99
00702273	Irish Songs	$14.99
00192503	Jazz Classics for Easy Guitar	$16.99
00702275	Jazz Favorites for Easy Guitar	$17.99
00702274	Jazz Standards for Easy Guitar	$19.99
00702162	Jumbo Easy Guitar Songbook	$24.99
00232285	La La Land	$16.99
00702258	Legends of Rock	$14.99
00702189	MTV's 100 Greatest Pop Songs	$34.99
00702272	1950s Rock	$16.99
00702271	1960s Rock	$16.99
00702270	1970s Rock	$24.99
00702269	1980s Rock	$16.99

00702268	1990s Rock	$24.99
00369043	Rock Songs for Kids	$14.99
00109725	Once	$14.99
00702187	Selections from O Brother Where Art Thou?	$19.99
00702178	100 Songs for Kids	$16.99
00702515	Pirates of the Caribbean	$17.99
00702125	Praise and Worship for Guitar	$14.99
00287930	Songs from *A Star Is Born, The Greatest Showman, La La Land*, and More Movie Musicals	$16.99
00702285	Southern Rock Hits	$12.99
00156420	Star Wars Music	$16.99
00121535	30 Easy Celtic Guitar Solos	$16.99
00244654	Top Hits of 2017	$14.99
00283786	Top Hits of 2018	$14.99
00302269	Top Hits of 2019	$14.99
00355779	Top Hits of 2020	$14.99
00374083	Top Hits of 2021	$16.99
00702294	Top Worship Hits	$17.99
00702255	VH1's 100 Greatest Hard Rock Songs	$34.99
00702175	VH1's 100 Greatest Songs of Rock and Roll	$34.99
00702253	Wicked	$12.99

ARTIST COLLECTIONS

00702267	AC/DC for Easy Guitar	$16.99
00156221	Adele – 25	$16.99
00396889	Adele – 30	$19.99
00702040	Best of the Allman Brothers	$16.99
00702865	J.S. Bach for Easy Guitar	$15.99
00702169	Best of The Beach Boys	$16.99
00702292	The Beatles — 1	$22.99
00125796	Best of Chuck Berry	$16.99
00702201	The Essential Black Sabbath	$15.99
00702250	blink-182 — Greatest Hits	$17.99
02501615	Zac Brown Band — The Foundation	$17.99
02501621	Zac Brown Band — You Get What You Give	$16.99
00702043	Best of Johnny Cash	$17.99
00702090	Eric Clapton's Best	$16.99
00702086	Eric Clapton — from the Album Unplugged	$17.99
00702202	The Essential Eric Clapton	$17.99
00702053	Best of Patsy Cline	$17.99
00222697	Very Best of Coldplay – 2nd Edition	$17.99
00702229	The Very Best of Creedence Clearwater Revival	$16.99
00702145	Best of Jim Croce	$16.99
00702278	Crosby, Stills & Nash	$12.99
14042809	Bob Dylan	$15.99
00702276	Fleetwood Mac — Easy Guitar Collection	$17.99
00139462	The Very Best of Grateful Dead	$16.99
00702136	Best of Merle Haggard	$16.99
00702227	Jimi Hendrix — Smash Hits	$19.99
00702288	Best of Hillsong United	$12.99
00702236	Best of Antonio Carlos Jobim	$15.99

00702245	Elton John — Greatest Hits 1970–2002	$19.99
00129855	Jack Johnson	$17.99
00702204	Robert Johnson	$16.99
00702234	Selections from Toby Keith — 35 Biggest Hits	$12.95
00702003	Kiss	$16.99
00702216	Lynyrd Skynyrd	$17.99
00702182	The Essential Bob Marley	$16.99
00146081	Maroon 5	$14.99
00121925	Bruno Mars – Unorthodox Jukebox	$12.99
00702248	Paul McCartney — All the Best	$14.99
00125484	The Best of MercyMe	$12.99
00702209	Steve Miller Band — Young Hearts (Greatest Hits)	$12.95
00124167	Jason Mraz	$15.99
00702096	Best of Nirvana	$16.99
00702211	The Offspring — Greatest Hits	$17.99
00138026	One Direction	$17.99
00702030	Best of Roy Orbison	$17.99
00702144	Best of Ozzy Osbourne	$14.99
00702279	Tom Petty	$17.99
00102911	Pink Floyd	$17.99
00702139	Elvis Country Favorites	$19.99
00702293	The Very Best of Prince	$19.99
00699415	Best of Queen for Guitar	$16.99
00109279	Best of R.E.M.	$14.99
00702208	Red Hot Chili Peppers — Greatest Hits	$17.99
00198960	The Rolling Stones	$17.99
00174793	The Very Best of Santana	$16.99
00702196	Best of Bob Seger	$16.99
00146046	Ed Sheeran	$17.99

00702252	Frank Sinatra — Nothing But the Best	$12.99
00702010	Best of Rod Stewart	$17.99
00702049	Best of George Strait	$17.99
00702259	Taylor Swift for Easy Guitar	$15.99
00359800	Taylor Swift – Easy Guitar Anthology	$24.99
00702260	Taylor Swift — Fearless	$14.99
00139727	Taylor Swift — 1989	$19.99
00115960	Taylor Swift — Red	$16.99
00253667	Taylor Swift — Reputation	$17.99
00702290	Taylor Swift — Speak Now	$16.99
00232849	Chris Tomlin Collection – 2nd Edition	$14.99
00702226	Chris Tomlin — See the Morning	$12.95
00148643	Train	$14.99
00702427	U2 — 18 Singles	$19.99
00702108	Best of Stevie Ray Vaughan	$17.99
00279005	The Who	$14.99
00702123	Best of Hank Williams	$15.99
00194548	Best of John Williams	$14.99
00702228	Neil Young — Greatest Hits	$17.99
00119133	Neil Young — Harvest	$14.99

Prices, contents and availability subject to change without notice.

HAL•LEONARD®

Visit Hal Leonard online at **halleonard.com**